This book... Acting, on Television.

Three Dimensional Acting for Two Dimensional Spaces

A Craft Book for Screen Actors.

by

Colin Bennett

Filament Publishing

Published by

Filament Publishing
14, Croydon Road,
Waddon, Croydon
Surrey CR0 4PA
0208 688 2598
info@filamentpublishing.com
www.filmentpublishing.com

© Copyright Colin Bennett 2006

ISBN 1-905493-11-8

Printed by CPI Antony Rowe Eastbourne

All rights reserved. No part of this publication may
be reproduced, stored in a retrieval system, or transmitted
in any form or by means of electronic, mechanical,
photocopying, recording or otherwise, without the
prior written permission of the publishers

Acting on Television, in the Movies, in Studios, on Location, in Commercials.

This book will tell you everything you need to know about bluffing your way onto the set as a professional actor.

These are the questions you were too afraid to ask.

These were the things they didn't teach you at drama school.

These are the tricks that get you the job from the audition.

These are serious ways to re-start your acting career.

These are some of the the ways to get auditions.

This is not a pretentious book on 'acting.'

This is the plumber's guide to acting.

Real rules, real world, real tricks and tips.

Warning!

This book is for actors only. Directors, casting directors, producers, techies, designers, researchers are not allowed to dip into this pool of acting secrets.

This is stuff we actors must keep from the rest of the world!

This book of secrets is dedicated to my family.

I thank them along with

Andy Warhol, Paul Aitken, Alan Rickman, Chris Day, Polly Hootkins, Richard Evans, Corinne Rodriguez, Paul De Feitas CDG, Jill Pearce, John Messenger, Peter O'Toole, RADA, Alan J W Bell, Keith Cheetham, Anthony Hopkins, Charlize Theron, Tom Jackman, Bruce Willis, Geoff Young, Roger Moore, Adam Knight, Peter Bourke, Lord Bernard Miles, Christopher Pilkington, Michael Dolenz, Lesley Powell, Warren Breach, Ken Cheeseman, Carol Groves, Woody Allen, Becky De Souza, BAFTA, Roy Kinnear, Francesca Greene, Paddy Ferrall, Peter Sellars, Philip Headley, Humphrey Bogart, Colin Prockter, Ingrid Bergman, Al Pacino, Jeremy Lee, Frazer Ashford, Wayne Sleep, Chris Hayes, Sally Power, Tony Hart

and to everyone
who has been on my TV courses and
to ALL Casting Directors everywhere.

And all the others who are on my list...
but whose names I can't read because of my
hand writing, sorry.

Thanks.

Foreword by Chris Hayes

I've have known and worked with Colin Bennett for more years than I care to remember. He is hard working and diligent and, as far as I know, very honest and highly suitable for the job for which he is applying.

He is bound to be a great asset to your company. But his brain is incorrectly wired, so you might find this book a right pain in the butt, but it is also very informative.

I agree with his opening remarks which clearly state that it is for new actors. Others might find it a difficult read. He cannot finish a sentence properly and he is constantly reminding us that he knows nothing. This is not true. He knows something.

There is no job he hasn't done in the theatre from cleaning the toilets to playing the saxophone. There is no job he hasn't done in the TV industry from being a floor manager to starring in cult classic skateboarding championships.

None of this gives you a true picture of who he is since he doesn't take a good photo. Don't hold that against him. He had very little formal education. He has earned a good living in a tough business with hardly any kind of discernible ability.

Though he can write quickly.... which is why I have allowed him to write my foreword... I'm a bit busy this week. I might regret letting him do it... don't worry I'll see it when I return from Rio.

Chris Hayes, famous theatre and TV director.

Introduction:

I doubt if I am well enough qualified to write this book. But then I would be suspicious of anyone who said they were!

We could ask Peter O'Toole to write it, after all he is, in my opinion, a great actor, very experienced at performing in front of the camera, and no doubt has some great advice to give but.... But, his first piece of advice might be `star in a pivotal movie, whilst still young, and be very beautiful.'

Since then his advice might be to make sure that your international agent shields you from most of the terrible scripts that get sent to you. He is a star and has always been so. For him the process is so easy that he just does it!

The rest of us actors, those who are not beautiful and are still waiting to star in their pivotal movie or TV series or indeed haven't yet been a visiting pathologist in The Bill wonder how the heck do you join the club?

This book is written specifically for actors who are occasionally invited to visit the club, (I have done my couple of visits as a pathologist in The Bill) but have never been on the real list.

This book, is a stream of hippie consciousness that I've done my best to arrange in some kind of order but acting is not a science. Indeed, I don't even believe that science is a science so there is little hope of stumbling upon a formula that will get you into full time regular employment as an actor let alone a screen star.

However, this wonderful `business' that we call `show' is just that, it is a business, more than that it is an industry, therefore it must have some predictable modes of operation. Most things that are predictable can be anticipated, anything that can be anticipated can be ambushed. The determined have to find a way of cutting the wagon train off at the pass, and join it before they are caught and thrown off again!

I am not a great actor, I might not even be a successful actor but I've earned a very good living in a very tough business for forty years. What I do feel I know... is a little of everything.

I started as a set builder and designer having left a technical school. Then I moved on to Drama School, first Rose Bruford followed by RADA, those were the sixties. I was a very successful theatre actor for the next ten to fifteen years or so, then I started writing, then directing, then producing, and then doing the same things for TV.

I tend to call myself a TV producer, now, if anyone asks. And I still do all of those jobs, if anyone asks. And it is from that stand point that I feel most qualified, to write this book. On my TV sets no-one is allowed to say, 'You can't do that!' Because I always know a way that we CAN do that!

TV producing, for me, brings all those strands together. It is perhaps from the POV of the producer that you really see how this business gets put together. So let us begin.... What's the POV?

I like glossaries and I think you should read the one at the back of the book But read it through and then dump it, no one expects actors to know all that stuff...

In fact I think it makes 'them' nervous that we know some of it. It gives them a feeling of security and superiority to call for a 246, or discuss 'Crossing the Line.' The business has changed: all those BBC people who used to think that actors lived in Gypsy encampments at the edge of town are now just as insecure as we always have been.

I think we should have a rough idea of their techno talk just to know that we needn't be intimidated by it! I'll make clear any stuff that you really should know. Sorry to insult the name of the Romany People by associating them with actors. Some actors are really nice people as are some Romany people.

A POV incidentally is 'Point of View.'

Forgive me if I write too much stuff that you already know! I know you know some of it but if you are not sure, best to read it here than ask. We must never let them know that we too are making it up. Incidentally, this book is only for Actors and maybe some writers.

Producers, Directors, Casting Directors, Camera People, and Technicians in General are not allowed to read this book. (though I'm unlikely to sue) It will give them glimpses into a secret world, which actors must try to keep as a `Mystery' to ourselves. It is best that `they' don't know what we do and how we do it.....

The book is basically divided into rough sections:

The Commercial

Corporate Work

TV Drama

How do you get the Work?

Comedy

Writing

and other stuff.

Chapter One

I'll start with How do you get the work?

Think logically, think like a business. We live in a world that increasingly demands specialisation. The Terms Director and Producer for example, sometimes to the outside world seem synonymous.

They are not, they are as different as Sound Recordist and Dancer. And just as the average Director almost needs permission to look through the camera, the Camera Person is unlikely to comment on the quality of the acting.

In very rough terms, the Producer gets the money, the Director spends the money. Your most important contact is the Casting Director. Everything I write can be denied or discussed but in general I'll try not to lie to you.

So if we need a dancer, sound recordist, camera person, carpenter, where will we find them? Well, they all needed to be trained. Whilst not being a member of Equity or having had a training at RADA or Guildford won't stop you from having a career as an actor, people will take you infinitely more seriously if you are a member of Equity and have had a training.

This book is really for people who have already gone further than that stage but I mention it simply because there are good working actors out there who have cut across the corner. We all have the right to try and work in our chosen area, we may not make it but we had the right to try.

Get a training of some sort, show dedication to improving your skills. If we are looking to cast actors then, in general, we want to know that you are a real actor, rather than someone with an un-defined talent waiting to be discovered.

So....?

Who does the Casting?

Who is looking for actors?

The Casting Director is your first port of call. If THEY don't know who you are then NO-ONE will know who you are. No one has ever got a commercial without first being suggested by a Casting Director. They may not make the final decision but they put the first lists together. We need to get on the list.

The advantage to this is that just as acting is our job, knowing actors is their job! So you must never have fears about contacting them. They should need to know more actors. They may not want to know more actors, but that's too bad. You need them to know who you are.

Obviously you must contact them. If you are just about to leave Drama School then you must write to everyone listed as a Casting Director in `Contacts' (see the glossary) and invite them to your final productions. Most of them may already be going, but it doesn't hurt for them to hear from you personally.

Some of them might get slightly ratty round the edges by receiving three hundred letters from emerging actors, so it's not a bad idea to split the list into sections and each actor take a group. They will already have been written to by the School, but even so.... it's your name you need them to remember not The Central School of Speech and Drama's.

And don't be fooled into thinking that your colleagues will actually do the writing. When I left RADA we were not able to construct complete lists of Casting Directors. But we did divide all the Agents in `Contacts' and wrote to those on our list.... strangely, only those in my section actually came to the show!

Was my letter better then all the others? I doubt it, though they were hand written. Was I just lucky? I doubt it, I've only ever won a ten pound prize on the lottery. Did the Post Office lose all the other letters? Seems unlikely.

The agents that came were the ones that I knew I'd written to. I won't say much more about leaving Drama School because all the best ones do their best to ease you into knowing the right people.

But remember: No one wants you to be `rich and famous,' except you! So you must do it.

I shouldn't say `Rich and Famous.' It got me into a lot of trouble with Politically Correct Theatres in the early seventies, when I was quoted in the Papers as having that ambition. A particular theatre said they'd never employ me if that was my goal! It is and it isn't. It is just a metaphor for being a full time working actor. The money is good and if you work often enough eventually someone will recognise you in the street. It may only be five minutes of the promised 15 but it does make it worth while.

So all that Drama School stuff is now behind you, or maybe you missed it, and a few years have gone by, your children have grown up, you've been made redundant, somewhere along the road you missed a boat to Hollywood, or it all became too hard making ends meet..... or you keep being offered TIE tours (theatre in education) and you are getting too old to hump things into and out of a van all day, but you want to try again. You need to re-focus your career.

Or as, a friend of mine puts it... he seems to be paddling his canoe up quite a good river. He is working, earning sometimes, meeting nice people, but just feels that the river that Alan Rickman is canoeing up, might be more fun. How do you pick up your canoe and walk over to Alan's river and start paddling up it. It will be more dangerous, the water there runs faster and deeper, but.....

Let's go back to the Casting Directors. I know lots of them. They are very nice people. I've never met one I didn't like. They are not like us actors at all, they are much nicer. They tend to be very quiet, shy, retiring professionals who... and this is the important bit.... are on our side.

It seems hard to believe, I know. We think of them as the gate keepers to a career that should be ours if only they would remember us more often. They don't see it like that.

Their job is, in general, to put in front of the Producer and Director some actors that they feel most closely and easily could play the characters that are outlined by the writer in the script.

Their job is not to help you with your career, though they would be thrilled if they could, no doubt, but it's not the reason they are Casting Directors.

They are good at placing faces and names or at least good at being able to find that information.

So how do we get them to know us?

Some don't mind a phone call. After all they live in a very phone based business, they are on the phone all day, like agents, and it's easy to say, NO, and put the phone down. It doesn't take a stamp or polite letter and the matter is either ended or you get invited to meet them.... but either way... unless you know that a particular Casting Director is happy with phone calls.. then I would never do it. Maybe I'm not pushy enough, maybe you are, you have to make that call for yourself... but don't tell them that I said you could!

Pushy is sometimes seen as a basic essential for being an important actor.... it isn't. Most of the best actors are not pushy, they have pushy agents but that's another story.

You have to write. But how do you get your letter read more carefully than the other 300 letters that they received that week. Or three thousand letters if they have just appeared in PCR! (The newsletter of forthcoming productions) Any successful business, TV Programme, invention, pop song has to have a hook! That one line description that says all you need to know to book to see the movie or not.

This is important! Don't enclose a tea bag or bar of chocolate, with the wish that they can enjoy a cup of tea whilst reading your CV. This is instantly binned. no-one in their right minds is going to eat a squashed sweet from a stranger, life it too tough. It is forgetting the first fact that we are all professionals. They are professionals they cannot be bought for the price of a PG Tip. And they will resent you trying. There is one Casting Director who says he doesn't mind... but he just keeps them to make him laugh... and show his casting director friends at dinner parties to which I'm not invited. He doesn't use them to cast Hollywood Movies.

I guess I should also point out that every Casting Director is different. And there are no rules but it does make sense that you follow what might be seen as a professional approach rather than pick yourself out of the crowd by signalling that you have just walked in off the street, and don't know how to behave. So phone if you are brave or send a letter.

What are you going to put in your letter?

The hook, the facts and a photo.

The hook is, why I have written to you? There has to be a reason, and it shouldn't be because I've been out of work for three years! Here are some simple ones but don't forget they've read them all.... you must look for your own unique, but professional reason.

1) I've just returned from three years in Dubai so you may not remember me....

2) My family have all grown up, thank goodness, and now....

3) You might have thought that I now only work in Hollywood but I'm home and...

4) I doubt if you will remember me but we met at....

5) I just had some new photos done and thought...

6) What do you think of the short hair in my new photos....? (no, maybe not... don't put them under pressure to follow you up!)

7) I've been on tour with Gaslight for 6 years and now it's finished I thought...

8) As you may know I've been nursing the elderly for the last 10 years but...

These all sound slightly tacky out of context, well, I am slightly tacky, but you have to think up your own! I also believe that most Casting Directors know who I am. I might be fooling myself here but I've been around long enough that most of them might. So I will always assume that they know who I am and know what I've been doing... and then they might believe that they've heard of me and have heard that I stopped acting to write for TV or whatever. No reason why you can't make the same presumption unless you are 15 years old and have never left Glossop in your life.

So my letter might start with the words, As you know I've been busy Directing and Producing for the last year but...

Returning from another career will never go against you especially if it's Nursing and you'd like to go into Casualty! I'll return to this subject later.

But you have to have a reason! The best reason is always...

I'm in next week's Last of the Summer Wine, please watch out for me.

Trouble is this doesn't work unless you are actually in Last of the Summer Wine!

But always tell them what you are doing.... no one else will. You can ask if your agent will do a mail out for you, you might have to pay the postage and the photos but I still think you should do some yourself. This is a business based on nepotism, partiality or favouritism. Nepotism is really good, unless you don't know anyone, in which case it stinks.

I'm not talking about big nepotism, like offering to pay for them to spend the weekend in a Paris Hotel that you might happen to own. I'm talking about small nepotism where you send them a letter every year and after the third they start to recognise your name. If it's your postage, then you have a right that they should at least start to recognise your name and not just your agent's.

Some have said they like Christmas Cards, that's easy, but I feel that you can only send them to Casting Directors that you know. Keep it Business. They might not like getting 30,000 letters but it's business and it's their fault for being in Contacts. Getting 30,000 Christmas Cards might seem a bit sad.

The hook has to be your own personal reason for contact, don't make it a joke, or flippant, or bitter. Just the facts and a photo?

The facts are the CV. This is a tough one. Each Casting Director has their own way of wanting it laid out. But here is a summary of what mainly seems appropriate.

Obviously your name must predominate.... sometimes you'll find that your agent's name will be bigger. I guess that's fair if they are putting it together and sending it out but don't forget that they have 30 other people that are just as happy to promote. If you are putting it together then you must be the star of your own CV.

Realistic basic descriptions, hair, eyes, height etc... Age? Playing age?

Tough one... don't mention it. Leave the age and playing age to them! This book is about screen acting. Playing age is a theatrical concept, it requires makeup and acting. TV doesn't want to know. If the part is for a 30 year old then they want someone who they believe looks 30, and might actually be 30! Your Agent and the Casting Director should know your real age and then they might conspire to tell the Director something that he wants to hear.... but never play this game against the Agent or Casting Director. It will always back fire on you one day.

After all we need actors of all ages, not just young ones or old ones but any age in between. Once you have lied about your age... what happens when a part comes along for which you are the perfect age? Casting Directors have long memories and good note pads, and they don't like being fooled. Nearly all of them hate bad spelling by the way!

Sensible contact details. Your agent should be the first and possibly only contact on the CV. If you don't have one then put real personal contact details. But they have to work. No-one I've ever met has said they would hold it against an actor not having an agent but.... they do get cross if they can't get to you quickly and efficiently. They don't keep trying, they try once and move on. So the telephone number has to be one that a person answers on a regular basis. This could be the best reason to have an agent!

Very few Casting Directors will leave a message on a machine, because it leaves the ball in someone else's court, and they can't get on with the job. You'd be surprised how many people have got jobs simply because they were the first ones on the list to answer the phone! 'Spotlight,' of course, will undertake this job for you, if you don't have an agent.

It is also true to say that geography isn't a deterrent to the casting process. If you really do live in the shadow of Newcastle Ale, then you will be considered for certain jobs without any problem. But most casting is in London and your address is Manchester? It's not that they care where you live, or that your address makes some assumption about your acting. They know that if they invite 6 actors to London for one job then 5 actors will have paid out fares for nothing. You might say, 'I don't care, call me anyway.' They don't want you to waste valuable resources.

So they might move on to the next name on the list rather than give you the financial dilemma. If they thought you were absolutely right and would get the job then they would bring you down but you are making them make choices for you.

There is a case to be made for having a London address on your CV even if it is not yours, but don't tell them I said this. You must be able to be contacted efficiently.

Mention your basic training, and any further training you have been upon. You are allowed to hype this slightly and make it seem slightly better than it was but be careful. You would be surprised how easy it is to spot a fake. Incidentally, no one wants to know how many GCSE or GCEs or GNVQs you have. Acting as we will see later cannot be defined as an academic exercise. Though real training in Nursing or the Law or Farming or Bricklaying might suddenly become important depending on what parts they are casting.

I'd better admit at this point that my agent normally sends out my CV and normally writes it. That's fine. But sometimes people ask me to send them one for specific jobs... I will always re-write it to push it towards what they need. This normally happens in the Corporate Arena. I'll discuss this later but with regard to CVs if Mercedes Benz ask for my CV, which they did recently, I will make sure that I stress the work I've done for other Motor manufacturers. They like to know that you have expertise in certain areas... fake or real! In today's Word Processing environment it is the easiest thing in the world to re-write the CV for each enquiry, though I wouldn't expect my agent to do this.

The facts are also of course the list of jobs.

If you haven't done any, then you had better say why. If they are amateur shows then it is best to admit it. My life's work is maybe 20 pages long and I guess most actors of my age can claim that. No one needs to know that much about me!

The longer you make your CV the less work they will assume you have done! It is easy to spot padding. Just one page! One page only!

Group the work as TV, Theatre, Film, Radio, Corporate, Commercial or whatever. List the Part Played, the Name of the Piece, the Theatre, the Director. In columns so that the information is easy to read, and if you have more than one page's worth then ask yourself which bits are they likely to have seen or heard about. It is good to know that you have done TIE but they don't need to know that you have done six pages of TIE, be selective. Don't lie about anything that they could catch you on, because they will. If you were in Shakespere in Love as an un-named serf extra, then it might be dangerous to give your un-named serf extra a name and say you played, Sidney the Serf.

Do you mention Extra work?

Most casting Directors would be happy to know where you have come from.... but... they will assume that an extra is what you are! They won't dismiss you for having been an extra, they will be pleased to know that you have tried to improve your craft by watching the process close to..... but.... all due respect to some very fine Extras they are not seen as actors by many people in the business. They are treated differently, employed differently, paid differently, their job is entirely different and if you are hoping to lift your canoe out of that particular river don't tell too many people where you got your canoe!

People try not to be prejudiced... but once you know something... it's very hard to forget it... unless like me you have a terrible memory and... I've already forgotten what I was talking about. I'll talk later about how to learn lines very quickly incidentally, remind me later! I'll forget!

If you have a professional CV then most Casting Directors will recognise some, if not all, of the Directors names listed. Make sure that these names are of people that really do know you! You are only a phone call away from being found out. Having said that, I approve of lying a little. Acting is lying. Good acting is good lying and bad acting is bad lying, but let's not talk about the truth being he really is `Henry the Vee!'

Because he's not!

And at the bottom of the CV most people will list skills. One casting director once said to me that she would love to call, through the Spotlight CD-ROM, all the actors together in one room that said they could juggle, and see how many of them could! I used to be able to Juggle quite well, I was part of an act which juggled. I think it still says I can do it on my CD ROM entry.... I do hope she doesn't call me into a room with a load of other liars! Maybe I'll delete it from the next edition!

A friend of mine once said he could water ski.... could he heck as like!? He was never caught because the stunt skier did all the skiing shots, but he spent a very nerve racking three days in the sunshine in Cannes, praying.

I was asked could I horse ride? Well, my wife did pay for me to take lessons for my 40th birthday. I was never very good. I'm too much of an old hippie. If the horse wants to go that way, why should I care? I'm not actually going anywhere special. If the horse doesn't want to trot, well, I wouldn't either. This, I'm told, is not the way to get the horse to respect you and obey you. I don't need the respect of a horse. I don't even expect my sons to obey me... so a horse!? They bite people too, you know, they don't tell you that when you watch Hickstead!

That reminds me, (though I'll try not to put in too many anecdotes,) that Sir John, sitting on his horse was asked by the First Assistant, do you know what to do when we call 'action?'
Yes, dear boy, but does the horse?

So anyway...

I said that I couldn't ride a horse, luckily. The guy who did do the job had to ride a `police horse' through the West End rush hour! He did it perfectly but even he, who could ride, had second thoughts when the traffic started to build up in Wardour Street! And the metal horse shoes started slipping on a cobbley bit in the rain, between an articulated lorry and a brand new 7 series BMW. I didn't lose the job I got another part more suited to my soft, under belly of the south, up bringing.

Do you list all your accents? Can you really do them? I think I'll phone up next week and delete half of my list of accents. Sometimes, I pretend to come from Halifax to get Northern jobs.....

Where, in Halifax, did you go to school?

Erm, well not actually, Halifax. More Hebden Bridge.

Oh, I know that very well.

Well, I suppose you'd call it Mytholmroyd.

Oh, Where abouts?

Actually, I left there as quite a small child.

But you've retained your accent?

Ehy by gum! I'll certainly go to the foot of our stairs, though it may not be as pure after living in London and being trained at RADA.

My first agent, now sadly, in Agent Heaven, assuming that such a place could exist, used to constantly lie about me....
I've told them you have a great American Accent.
They are only interviewing real American's aren't they?
Yes, that's why I've told them that you are a real American!

So I go in `being' American.

So you are American?

Yep, well, half American, My mother was English and my father was American.

Where from?

Hollywood.

What was he?

(steady) He used to be part of the I love Lucy Team. (A lie too far)

Hey, I knew all those guys! What did he do?

(Long beat)

There was quite an acrimonious divorce, my mother never referred to him again.

I'm sorry I shouldn't have mentioned it!

s'OK.

I got the job. But I've always felt guilty!

Are you going to include your photo in with your CV?
Well normally you might.

Photos are a tricky subject!

It's easy to build a small thumb-nail into the printed sheet but if it's for a good job include a proper one.

Anything is acceptable and yet there is an expectation.

Here are a few photo rules that you can break...

It MUST ALWAYS be a Black and White, Glossy, Head shot, Looking directly into the camera, measuring 10 by 8. Without the name on the front, but with the name and phone number on the back.

Now you know the rules... you can break them.

Americans always have coloured photos. It doesn't tell you much more that you already knew. Indeed, you can spot American Photos a mile away and they don't sit well on a table of UK Photos. They are too glamourous. And we tend to pull back from Glamorous in the acting game. We believe that even non perfect people are allowed to be actors. In America these people are only allowed to be on Gerry Springer.

The one thing that all Casting Directors agree is that the photo should look like you! If you are glamourous then the photo can be glamourous. If you are not, then so should the photo. When they call you in for a casting they expect the person in the photo to come through the door, not her older less glamourous sister or for that matter not her younger plainer sister. But her!

How do you pick the photo? Marilyn Monroe was, we are told, loved by the camera. I am not, the camera thinks that I look like Punch. Maybe I do, but even Punch gets work. I am faced with 36 exposures on a contact sheet and I am lucky to get one frame from the page worth looking at... no problem there then, that's the one. But if you have six to choose from, where do you begin?

Ask your mother? No, she'll pick the pretty, young, vulnerable one.

Ask your Friend? No, she'll pick the one that puts her friend in the best light.

Ask your agent? Not bad, but they too have an agenda, they are looking for a cross section of talent.

Ask a neighbour? I think so. They can be objective. Not that I can ask mine, since I tried to build that shed without planning permission, and he blew the whistle on me with the local council... but maybe your neighbour, could be objective... ask them to pick the photo that most looks like you! (not me)

Glossy 10 by 8? No need. It could be a postcard.... not a passport, but a postcard mass produced would do, (if it's for a mail out) as long as you can clearly been seen. Glossy, who cares?

The point is this.... at some point all the photos will be placed on a table in front of the Director or Producer. There might be 15 Black and White glossy 10 by 8s. Yours might stand out if it is in colour.... could be good, could be bad, expensive certainly..... but if you are the only `non glossy passport photo' you are going to look like a cheapskate!

Sorry, but that's life. Horses for courses, photos for specific purposes, custom and practice, professional.

If it's a mail-out to say, 'I'll be a Clerk of Court on next Wednesday's The Bill,' then a postcard will definitely do. It can be saved or binned, You don't care and they are pleased to know that you don't care.

If it's a `first introduction' or in response to a requested photo then a 10 by 8 is best.

If it's just a mail out to remind them that you are still alive (don't use this as your hook, unless it has been in doubt) then a small but clear photo will do.

Shall I get my brother to take the photo?

Well, don't ask my brother, his eyes are going and he never answers the phone! I don't know what they get up to in that flat all day. But certainly get your brother to have a first go! Don't use these. Thank your brother or friend very much and say it was a very useful exercise but you are going to have them done down the High Street next time.

Use them for practice, to practice not acting for the photo! Practice looking straight into the lens. Practice with four different outfits, practice with your hair up or down , shaven or un-shaven, looking smooth or rough, standing, sitting, garden or studio.

Once you have done them down the High Street, you may still not be happy with them. If you are then great, if not.... go to Spotlight offices in Leicester Square and flick through Spotlight, just flick don't study yet... just flick.... and note the ones that stop you in your tracks! That's the kind you need. Not over acted, not cleverly lit, not a fine or stylish example of the photographer's art, but a face that you look at twice from a photographer who on the right day with a following wind might be able to do the same for you.

These guys are more expensive than your brother or the old boy down the High Street but you do need the real thing, pin sharp, well framed, clean and clear. Nothing trendy, they date too quickly. Most Casting Directors and Agents would like us to change our photos every year but life's too short. Just make sure it looks like you at your current age!

Shall we put our names on the front? My agent likes to do this, along with her Logo, so fair enough. But some people think it makes the photos look like `Variety' photos. If we are actors, and we must be specific, we don't want to look like `Variety' people, as nice as they are.

Shall we split it into quarters and show different aspects of our acting? No, I have done, me with glasses, without glasses, with moustache, without moustache... or even me with cigarette, me without cigarette.Don't do it.

It makes you look like a Walk-on, with your own wardrobe of policeman's uniforms, builders clothes, judges outfits etc. Have mobile home will travel. It really isn't what `real' actors do... and that's what we are trying to pretend to be. Let me stress that I say that with all due respect to Extras, Walk Ons and Background Artistes, they do another job.

Full face? Yes, don't pose 3/4 shots looking into the middle distance. It's difficult to make that seem real, mainly 'cos it isn't! Don't crop the photo below the hair line. We know your hair is thinning, the part may require that it is thinning, so let's not pretend that by cutting off the top of your head, we will be fooled into thinking that out of shot you look like Albert Einstein.

Don't wear a low cut top and then crop the photo to simply end in cleavage. It will make you look tarty. I suppose if you are tarty then that's good. But it might send out mixed signals and they'll call you in for the wrong reasons.

Important to remember, that if you have to do something sleazy to get the job then you'll get sleazy jobs! In the real world of TV and Films where real money is riding on the success or failure of the product, Producers and Directors and Stars find it safer to pay for sex rather than sleep with a terrible actor, who could ruin their film.

I don't know any that do pay for sex, by the way, that was just an example. They tend to only do that so that they can get caught, modify their image, and push the interest in a 'quiet movie' up the ratings. Though, as I say, I don't know any examples of this.

Always have your details on the back of the photo in case it gets separated from the CV, not in felt tip pen, directly on the back, as this can get rubbed off onto the face of your next photo! Be simple. Believe me as a director I have scanned the pages of Spotlight for hours looking for a face. And everyone does! You must be in there or you are nowhere.

All the above rules can be broken for whatever reason you can choose but what I'm really saying is you need to be spotted in the crowd.... but not because your photo is out of step with 'Custom and Practice.'

So that's the package, the hook, the facts and the photo. Now to send it out... there are probably 200ish Casting Directors in Contacts. You'll know some names, most you won't.

Where to begin?

Keep a book! Write in it things you have liked and who cast it. And start with them. Write in it any Casting Directors you meet and where. We would hope that they remember us, maybe we should make the effort to remember them! Make it look like a personal letter. Dear Corinne, etc... I think most Casting Directors would agree that this is a first name business, so use the name. Never, Dear Sir or Madam.

Never!!

We are in a business where we need to know people, like people, have relationships with people. Dear Sir or Madam is some other planet! I'm happy to call all the Casting Directors by first name, but then I'm old. If you are unsure of this, or feel uncomfortable with this, then you should say, Dear Jill Pearce (Complete Name) Don't try to second guess if they are Mz or Miss or Mr or Mrs, you'll get it wrong. Having said that, there are some I might try to be slightly more formal with, but what the heck you can't get it all right.

A friend of mine says that he writes a letter a day. Something that requires action from someone else. Can we manage one letter a day, 7 per week, 30 per month? By the end of the year you will have written 365 letters, that's all the Casting Directors with 165 left for some agents. Goodness knows how many agents there are? Spotlight will know and they may be able to help you find one whose books are not clogged up with very talented people who look just slightly better than you. It's a tough game, but no-one begged you to want to do it! In fact, if you wanted to do something really useful for the world you should go and work for Oxfam. We do it because we need to do it for ourselves. But you are allowed.

As a TV producer I know that I will never sell a TV programme to a broadcaster unless she reads my letter offering her 2 hours of Championship Skipping just after someone has said that they can no longer provide two hours of Mud Wrestling.

She puts the phone down, swearing, and picks up my letter and the problem is solved. Great, she gets two hours of Skipping.... think about it, it's not so bad, and I get to sell another cult narrow band interest sporting event. Which will disappear into the mists of time as if it had never been!

It is the same with actors. It's a number game.... At Encyclopaedia Britanica they say that you must collect 100 names and addresses in order to meet and talk to 10 families. You must meet and talk to 10 familles in order to sell one set of Encyclopaedia Britanica! So if a guy goes into the office and says,

Tough week I haven't sold a single set of books this week.

His boss says, how many names did you have on your list?

About 100.

How many families did you meet and talk to?

Well, it's been a tough week!

In other words you didn't do 10!

History has taught us that the take up rate was always about 1 in 100. It may not be anymore now that Technology has revolutionised the Encyclopaedia Business but it's probably still a numbers game. And you can't skip a street just because you think that no one in that street will want what you have to sell.... it's the numbers that count, like the lottery.... you might have 300 names without a single meeting and then three will come along together.

The God of numbers must be appeased. Having said that, don't get obsessed. We are not selling Encyclopaedia Britanica. A properly focussed addressed, written and spelt letter, with a reason for having been written, will always be spotted in the in tray over a Word Processed mail-out.

Casting Directors have a tough time too.

They have mortgages, cats, cars, fax machines, assistants, and need to eat. So maybe it's worth just a few words to work out what they want from us. They have to audition for jobs just as we do. A producer will ask them to compete with a couple of other Casting Directors to give an idea of how they might cast the current project.

Then the Casting Director might have a meeting to justify their proposal and modify the requirements and agree on whether the product can be cast for what's in the budget! Having got the job the focus of their professional day is simply in casting that product. They don't assemble stables of possible actors in the hope that one day they will need a one armed juggling Armenian.

They probably will keep that CV in their special skills tray but other than that they don't need actors.... until they need the specific actors required to fulfil that cast list. The timing of your contact to them is a lottery. But if God is on your side then occasionally your CV will arrive on the day that they are looking for someone just like you. And occasionally you'll pick six winning numbers. Yeah Right.

If not, what happens? It gets binned? Maybe eventually. If they kept every CV and Photo ever sent then they would never get any work done. They'd be too busy finding places to file them in. One famous Movie Casting Director used to like receiving CVs because she was able to re-cycle the paper clips before binning the CV and Photo! That sounds cruel but you must put yourself into the position of understanding it.

She would only cast major movies. So if she hadn't heard of you then there was no way you were going to get an interview for a major movie. QED. We have to work out sensibly where we fit into this business. Of course, always aim higher, but no-body owes us anything. Apart from the man who borrowed my lawn mower in 1956 and then left the district! But I wouldn't want to burden you with my problems.

So they have your CV and maybe there is something on it that catches their eye! If they are casting casualty and you once were a nurse, they'd like that!

But they might never cast you in anything if they are not sure you can act! So what can we do about that? Many Casting Directors set up regular general interview sessions where, maybe once a month or every two months, they'll set a day aside to meet some new actors. If they do then that's one good reason to write to them, to get on that list.

You mustn't try to trick them into making a response to you. If your letter contains a direct request that requires them to respond, you are backing them into a corner. They have two choices, either force themselves to spend a day a week writing, Thank you for your CV but.... letters.

Or dumping your letter in the bin without responding whilst still feeling guilty! Guilt is a terrible thing to put onto a stranger whom you were hoping to gain as a colleague! On the streets of London I have a rule. I give coppers to beggars, I give silver to Buskers and I always try to cross over the street to put money INTO the charity boxes being rattled. Why?

Not because I'm a compassionate person. In fact, you can face a certain amount of a abuse giving a beggar three pence! I don't do it for them but for me. If I don't do it, then I spend the next ten minutes feeling guilty. I don't need guilt, I'm basically a good person, well... not a very good person... but... well, anyway... If they want to earn their living by begging... I wouldn't want to do it... but what else am I going to do with loose copper change, it buys me a clear conscience.

Some would say don't give Beggars anything, some might say, three pence is not enough to buy a cup of tea.... I say.... I've forgotten now. Though tea sounds like a good idea. But I don't want to be dogged by guilt! Just like acting, make choices.

No-body owes you anything. A letter or an acknowledgement? You choose to write, you have to be prepared not to be noticed. But if they do notice you, they still might not know if you can act.. they need to see you in something. I'll talk more about this later but if they are placing their professional judgement on what you can do then they have a right to know that you can do it!

Maybe they caught your 'man in van' or your 'woman in the supermarket' in Eastenders... so they know that someone has employed you! This is a bigger step than you might suppose.

Why do we keep seeing the same old faces on the box all the time? Are we short of actors? You might be forgiven for thinking that all older women are played by Dame Judi Dench and men are played by Geoffrey Palmer. And if they are busy... then we'll start to look for some footballers or presenters to see if they can hack it.

Did that sound bitter? I didn't mean it to.

One of the most Golden rules of our life is never be bitter!

Never.

It shows!

And it is not pretty!

And it doesn't help!!

I'm not!

OK, don't go on about it then.

The reason why we keep choosing the same actors is that we are in a high risk business. Judi Dench is a wonderful actor, a great actor, and we would be lucky to have her in our cast, and she will sell a few `tickets'... but more than this... we know she will hack it! New people will be given a chance but one has to realise that `they' (and I'm not talking about Casting Directors in this case) are frightened about the future as are we. In fact, more worried than we are!

They have gone and acquired bigger mortgages than us! bigger cars, better holidays, more PEPs and much more expensive mobile phone packages, than us Gypsies. Sorry, Gypsies again. I mean no disrespect , some actors like collecting old cars too. Oh, and by the way, I do have several big houses... but I've just been lucky.

When I am given a chance to direct, I firstly think about my friends and colleagues. it's right and proper! But most of them will make their excuses, say they are busy. They know I'm a cheapskate and I will want them to load the lorry, do wardrobe, check the sound, buy the tape stock, as well as play Uncle Vania... so then I must look further afield. Then I call in a Casting Director.... and the real process begins... and she tells me that it's OK for them to load the lorry, though they may want more money, but it's unfair to make them buy the Video stock!

Life's tough! Ignore the last paragraph it was just plain silly and misleading... but often true.

In fact, don't let's pretend that TV is lucrative. It isn't. My daily rate for an appearance in Last of the Summer Wine is what I would earn for a week in the theatre. The difference is that you are rarely employed for less than seven weeks in the theatre but lucky to get three days on Last of the Summer Wine! And it's not much more than the BEEB used to pay me 15 years earlier! It's hardly a living either way. So who's making the money? Let me put it into perspective for you.... it's business.

Why do we now make three hours of The Bill and four episodes of The Street and maybe a total of three to six episodes, including repeats, of `The Square?' It's business. And it's going to get tougher. TV drama is closing down into a smaller area of Top Budget Classics for world sales and long running Soaps. Just for the record, The Bill doesn't classify itself as a soap. Because we never get to see where Sgt Cryer lives. I do, because he's my nephew! Though we only get to see them once a year at Christmas. He's obsessed by motorbikes! And you can't get a lamb chop there for love nor money.

We will soon destroy our own television industry, like we did with our movie industry, in the mythical search for competition driven cost cutting. Like we may do with the NHS. It's like trying to pay actors in relation to productivity. it doesn't work, anymore than trying to pay nurses for productivity, it is patent nonsense, but some desk bound suited dork, who couldn't act his way out of a paper bag thinks it makes economic good sense.

Let me take a few moments out to get cross.

Years ago someone decided that it was `wrong' for the two major companies to make movies and own picture houses. Even though it ensured a secure and future proof cinema industry. So the major picture house owners had to dump their cinemas or their production arm. The industry collapsed. It wasn't just the fault of the 'Carry on Movies,' though they were terrible and not very funny or much loved on their first trip around the cinemas. It is only time and nostalgia that has given them a sheen of `weren't they cute in the olden days' feel.

We knew what a great movie was then, just as we do now. The fact that Benny Hill is so big in the states doesn't mean that the average UK viewer didn't shrug and pretend it wasn't happening at the time. Whilst we were trotting out `Carry on Movies' the Americans were making Cape Fear! And even earlier whilst we were trotting out George Formby movies they were making Astaire and Rogers epics. But the British movie industry collapsed for more reasons than just that we made rotten films. When we get to talking about real acting I'll come back to this but for the moment let's look at the UK TV market.

The same thing that happened in movies is happening now, each franchise area is forced to compete on a regular basis to maintain their licence to transmit to any given region. These are awarded on the basis of a `Quality Threshold.' You and I, naive as we are, might assume that the quality they referred to was quality in programme making. Wrong. They were referring to quality of business plan. What the heck does that mean... basically who can produce more TV Hours per shareholders profits than their competitors....

So brilliant TV companies Like TVS disappear and Mediocre Publishing cash cows companies like C.......... turn up. They are starting to get better, but boy have we waited a while.

LWT kept their franchise for something like 72 million pounds... Central kept theirs for the price of a second hand Cortina, in poor condition with three months MOT.

There might be more to that than meets the eye but I'm sure I can't comment, I can't afford to be sued!. Let me stress categorically that I don't believe that anything underhand went on in the awarding of franchises. Nothing, absolutely not. I have no doubts about this, no, none! Please, there is no more to be said! I absolutely deny that my writing this simple anecdote, the truth of which I have absolutely no insider knowledge, implies any wrong doing.

Where was I, oh yes, being naive
.
Then having won their franchises on whatever criteria, sensible or stupid, they are allowed to sell these to the highest bidder!

So that TV companies that were set up to address local television needs are now being run from the other end of the country. And soon, these franchises will be allowed to be bought by foreign TV companies, with hardly any regulation at all. We, of course, in the UK will prohibit UK TV Companies from buying into continental regions because...... well, I have no idea. Sorry.

Whilst my blood pressure is at a dangerously high level I'll just give you a simple example of where TV is heading. And then I'll go and take four of my, 'take one tablet per day with meals' pills. I take them for medical reasons... They make me feel old and tired but my doctor assures me that this is better than feeling really well and then suddenly dying. it's a close call, but... anyway.

A few years ago, in the olden days when independent TV Producers were.... well, independent. I would be able to phone up LWT and ask if they would like to buy thirteen hours of Skateboarding or Snow Boarding. In those days 'buying' meant that they bought the rights to show the programmes twice over a period of say two years and then they would give the master tapes, or transmission tapes, back to me. It was in all senses of the word my programme.

Meanwhile, of course I could also sell the programme to anyone else who wanted it, Anglia or TVS or shorts clips from the `Championship Finals' to Trans World Sport for inclusion into their weekly magazine format. Life was good then, life was still tough but it was all possible.

So I find 13 hours of Championship Pool Competition and offer it to LWT, the man he say, Yes! I then offer it to Sky Sports and the man he say, Yes, but I need 30 hours!

Great, With a few more three camera OB set ups, it's easy. There are literally hundreds of Pool matches going on simultaneously, the more tables you feature, the more hours of TV you can produce. Also one has to say that though top Pool players can make the game look about as exciting as watching paint dry, it is very easy to shoot. Here's the table.... this is where the balls will be, so let's just shoot what happens here.

Mountainbike Championships are more difficult!
Where the heck is everyone?
On the other side of the mountain!
Maybe we had better move over there?
By then they will be over here!
Oh, bugger. Can anyone lend me any Wellington boots?

Then I Phone Sports Channel America, do you want 30 hours of Pool?

Yep, sure do. Any American Players?

No problem! (at the time I might have had to drag them out of RAF Upper Heyford which is where we shot the Skipping, though they are all closed down now) But no problem! Some might even be quite good, though you'd never know it!

Now let's talk money.

LWT will pay 2500 per episode, for 13 episodes, at the time this would have been just enough to pay for the OB facilities, and some of the editing.

Sky Sports?
Hi, Do you still want my 30 hours of Pool, it now includes some Top American Players?
T'riffic!
How much are you paying? I ask.
Money! You want money???!!! No, I'll show it if you give it to me!
Oh, right, thanks.

Sports Channel America?
Hi, Do you still want my 30 hours of Pool, we have some great US International Players. You might not have heard of some of them but they seem to be better known in Europe (That part of Europe we call Oxfordshire)
That's right on the button!
Good, Let's talk money. I ask.

OK, the deal is you send it to me on One hour tapes, NTSC, 6 `black slugs' per hour for me to drop in my ad breaks. And it will cost you $5000 per hour.

I pay him! I pay him?
Yep He wants me to pay him to show my programme!

A few years ago I sold a series of TV products to `Channel TV' and they paid me 1 (that's one pound) per episode! How I long for those good old profitable days.

If you read Televisual, which I do, the regular magazine for TV professionals, though I suppose I'm more of a hobbyist than a professional, you can read that the 30 second Title sequence for a certain show was made in Soho for 150,000, shot on.... edited on... mastered on.... rendered by... 3D'd with.... sweetened by... etc.... etc... fiddled endlessly in...

It's all Emperor's Clothes. The title sequence may have cost that, but they make 4 episodes of show per studio day! With the audience changing seats for each episode. In the real world broadcasters are paying less and less for the product, and independents are getting less and less independent. And it's always been tough to be an actor. You know this... but it's worth you knowing a bit about why. And soon everything will be sponsored.

So don't assume that you are being ripped off by the producer. In the real world of TV, in which there are literally millions of hours of crap... sorry historic repeats... yet to be screened. It is not easy to get new stuff made. Sorry, I'll just go and lie down for a while then I'll be back with the casting Directors again.

That's better.

Right. If they have anything that suits you, in their opinion, at that moment in time, then they may want to see you, meet you, have you meet the director. And a new bond in the business will have been made. Incidentally, (you might have to go to their offices which might be in their house)

When you get to have a meeting with them,

come early,

not too early,

don't knock on the door of a private residence more than 5 minutes before the allotted time,

don't instantly ask for the loo or a cup of something,

don't make yourself too at home.

Casting Directors don't get off on the power they wield, but you must know where to draw the line between `best chums forever, let's always keep in touch' and `colleagues that pass in the day.' Just as they are not looking for the odd squashed chocolate, they are not looking for pen pals! They don't want to feel stalked! Don't write in coloured inks!!!!

Enough already, let's move on to a Commercial Casting.

I'm going to be very specific now about a casting, not an audition. A casting is normally when a Casting Director has found your photo or remembered you from a play at the Kings Head in 1972 and thinks that you are just right for the next Oxo family. You and 500 others!

It starts with a call to your agent or your sister, who is pretending to be your agent, because she has a London address. Or a call to your home in the Lake District where you have vowed always to go to London, if called, no matter what the expense. If you don't have an agent then your entry in Spotlight can be c/o of Spotlight, no-one will think the worse of you, as long as you can be contacted at short notice.

The request from your agent normally says, can she be in Old Compton Street at 10 o/clock tomorrow morning to be seen for the part of a business woman? Not much to go on but you must get more.

Ask if the appointment can be later, so that you can use a cheap day return, if you live in Yorkshire. They won't mind and will change it if they can. Don't change it if you don't need to!

These things are difficult enough to put together at short notice. If you can't go... then just say you would have liked to but you can't go. Simple. Then forget that they ever made the call. Move on. If you CAN make it...

Find out more, from your agent, about the business woman. What kind, what age, what class, what.....?

They may not know anymore than that but...

The Casting Director WILL have given your agent as much information as they have.

They might also ask if you are prepared to take the daily rate of .... and are you free for the shoot days which will be between.....?

This is a difficult one, they are negotiating before you get the job... but there is no way round it... agree to the money, I would... that's what they think it's worth. If you think that you are exactly what they are looking for and they would be lucky to find anyone as good then hold out for better money. But don't hold your breath. There 30,000 other actors who'd do it for nothing, including me! And frankly the money on a long running ad is very good by any standards. Don't tell anyone what you are getting.

Golden Rule.... never discuss money with anyone apart from your agent.

Never discuss it with other actors.

Never.

It will always end in tears.

One of you will be smug and one of you will feel exploited. You never know which one it will be in advance. It is not worth knowing. We all get paid differently. This may not be so in communist countries, assuming there are any. But I would rather take the risk of earning slightly more than my friends than working full time at a universal rate to do plays dictated by the State!

[Illustration: Two market-stall vendors shouting, with boxes labelled "GOOD ACTORS 10 per penny!" and "GREAT ACTORS 9 per penny!"]

I don't want to sound like a management toady but be glad you know someone who employs actors. be glad you have been offered a casting, be glad you don't have to take a pill every day to keep your blood pressure steady. Be glad you are not me. Though, I do drive the most beautiful car in the world and live in a wonderful house, with automatic garage doors, and have a cottage by the coast. But you don't know the price I have paid, he said sadly, though with a slight twinkle in the eye.

Are you free on the shoot days?

Be honest! If you are not it could be dangerous. If you are not free to do the 2 or 3 shoot days don't go to the casting! Don't go just for the practice (Though you could go if it was for a musical in the theatre, it's always worth rehearsing your songs with a free pianist, but that's another business) If you go and get the commercial and then tell them that you are not free on the shoot days they might sue you for the cost of the casting session!

Really?
I promise, it's true.
Has it happened to you?

Actually, I was offered a job by fax whilst I was at the casting for the commercial, I had already semi-agreed to do the fax job... so I only learnt about it when I got home to find that I had been offered both jobs. The fax job had got in first, but I had gone to the casting...
It got very tense for a while, and upset several people that I would not have upset for the world. It worked out in the end but it cost me. Just be careful, these sessions are costly for all of us, but most of all for the people setting it up.

So you know where to go and when. Good, now get there 45 minutes early. I used to be very lucky with parking meters in London. They are a dying breed. I still go by car (you know why,... I like pedestrians in Wardour Street to think I'm a Hollywood Producer, or at the very least a Porn distributor from Holland) I now park my car in the Multi stories because if you know where they are, then it's easy, expensive but easy. But by the time you add the train, the tube, the coffee, the risk of being mugged against the car.... I'm afraid the car still wins.

I now admit the Old Age Freedom Bus/train/tube Pass beats all comers!! But I'll still be there 45 minutes early. Why?

Because, if you are not 45 minutes early, then you're late! How come?

Well, people throw themselves under trains. Not only actors, but real people. That will delay the train and you'll be late. Excuses, excuses... "Someone threw themselves under my train." They might say, Oh, were they on the casting list?
No, it was just a real person!
Oh, pity, we were looking for some real people.

But more likely they will have heard that excuse before and think, This is someone who can't get up 45 minutes earlier than the last possible moment!

It takes 45 minutes to be on time.
It only takes 15 seconds to be late.
You might still be late... if World War Three breaks out for example but then this casting will be the least of your worries.

Not for me, of course I'm too old to be any good as a soldier but I'll do all the acting whilst the young people are away. So let's not dismiss it out of hand.

But there are several other more compelling reasons to be early.

You'll be able to read the script, calm down, relax and know that you have the moral high ground, because they will be running late. It doesn't matter. Ask yourself, would I like to earn say 10,000 for two days work? If the answer is no, then you are probably the MD of a major public utility and shouldn't be trying to take work from poor actors. If the answer is yes, then also ask yourself what am I prepared to do to get this job?!

I'm not talking sleaze here, I'm talking preparation. I doubt if anyone should go to central London wearing a Chicken outfit, unless they work for KFC. But there is a case to be made that you needn't make it difficult to spot that you are right for this job! Always dress for the part.

Always?

No.

Give an indication. Don't wear a nurses uniform.... but wear a plain dark blouse with a white collar, straight skirt.... I'm talking about a casting for a nurse by the way not a builder. If it's for a builder, don't wear a boiler suit and hard hat but wear a working shirt and jeans. Don't wear a policeman's uniform but wear black trousers, white shirt, official club kind of tie, dark blazer. It's all a game....

Let's think about this for a while....

I wrote a play recently about the discovery of Anaesthetics for UCH. It was performed with professional actors for the hospital's anniversary of the event. Apart from the real actors playing the leading scientific heroes of the Victorian Era we needed a chorus of players to give us a quick montage of major medical innovations through the ages.

It wasn't going to last long... 30 seconds of name, date and discovery... a montage of facts... we got the chorus, we needed about ten people, they were played by anaesthetics students. These are very clever young people, dedicating their lives to medicine, their learning, their intellect, their ability to assimilate scientific facts beyond doubt. A team of them would have thrashed a team of us, at University Challenge or probably anything. But the paper bag appeared and they couldn't act their way out of it!

If it were possible to make commercials with real people then that's who they would choose, because they are cheaper, don't demand a living wage, are pleased to help, thrilled to be on TV... etc.... but the fact is, we have a definitive skill. And so they have to have actors pretending to be real people.

But they would prefer real people.

So you must look like what it says in the script. It sounds obvious doesn't it, but for years I'd go to castings looking like me..... and never getting any.

In the script... it might say:

Unemployed actor walks into the room.

If you are an unemployed actor, then that's what you'll look like in your real life.

I'm not sure what I look like, certainly nothing easily defined. (I'll be more specific later in talking about real acting) They don't want you as you look in real life. Think about it, how often do you see people on the streets wearing jeans?... then think about how often people wear jeans on TV.... only in jeans commercials!

I thought I'd make it easy for them.

In any group of men there are the beer drinkers, (not me) the intellectuals (not me) the fat slobs (not me) the clerks (not me) the skinny hippies (maybe once, but not really) so I decided to be the one who wears the very thick bottle bottom glasses. Slightly eccentric (starting to sound close) but in all other respects looks normal.

That's when I started to get commercials. I wasn't cheating them, I was just showing them something positive.

It's important to remember that I wore the glasses the moment I got into the room with the director. Not before and not once I was in front of the camera. But I literally put them on as I passed from the waiting room into the inner sanctuary!

Why not put them on in the waiting room?

Because every other actor would think, that's a good idea, and put his funny glasses on! We are all playing the game, some are better than others and it has little to do with acting in the Stanislavski sense. Though I will get around to that too.

There were many jobs I wouldn't get by being the short sighted person, but I got the ones who were! I know it's true, because, I was cast to play a vicar, I think it was, who sang, Bar bar bar, bar bar of Club. (the Beach Boys were responsible for many of my award winning commercials) At the wardrobe fitting in the West End three days before the shoot, I wasn't wearing my glasses. I wasn't expecting to see the director. He was there, his face dropped half a mile when he saw me, his only words were....

You have got your glasses haven't you?

I whipped them out of my pocket,

put them on and the panic was over.

He had cast the right actor!

God punished me shortly afterwards. When I hit 40 he gave me an old person's eyes, which seem to require thicker and thicker glass! The ones I wore at Castings weren't real!

I currently play my, old responsible guy in suit, who could be a pathologist, at castings unless it specifically says something else.
In fact, it seems in my life, these days, I mainly go about disguised as a much older person.

Read the script!

It looks simple enough, One page, the images are on the left and the voices are on the right. Actors tend to read what's on the right, think that's simple enough and then go back to chatting to the guy next to them that they haven't seen for years and thought was dead. Commercial Castings are great, if they need someone like you then they will need to see 20 guys like you. Put in room with 20 Equity members that are like us, (same age, class, region etc) and quite a few of us will know each other! Time to chat about who has gone to the great Green Room in the sky, etc... but don't! Have a chat, maybe meet for Coffee later, but make sure you have read that script. Understood it, thought it through.

I guarantee that 20 minutes after you did your bit for the camera you will suddenly think.... Oh, Yes, I see now what they were after! If I could go back and have another go I'd get it right! Too late. If you know that's true, if you've done it, been there, got the tee shirt, then you won't need me to remind you. So if you start the process 20 minutes earlier then you might get to do it right... when it is required.

Don't be frightened to change, even at the last minute. Everything that it says in the script has been agreed over months through tedious meetings with the client, the director, the producer, the account manager, the agency, the coffee person, the demographic experts, the ITC, Mr Kipling his wife etc... So what it says on the script is what they want to see. Think about it. I'll write it again because it's important....

What it says on the script is what they want to see.

`Man shaving, in bathroom, wearing a vest and pyjama bottoms discovers a pregnancy testing kit'

If you had come in your pyjama bottoms they would think you were a looney. On my casting day, several actors had been into Mark's on the way in and bought a new vest.

They still have them in cellophane bags, possibly with pins hiding all over them.

I'd forgotten to buy a new vest... I sit in a room with actors that I know quite well, slowly metamorphosing into what it says in the script. none of them wants to draw attention to himself in case there is a rush for the bathroom with the plastic bags of vests.! I wait, I nod, I smile... as I'm called into the room, just as I leave the sight of the other actors I slip out of my shirt and arrive bare chested......

Most of us actors think that we can do almost anything, it comes with the territory. And so we know we can do bare chested acting, hairy chested acting, smooth chested acting, big chested acting, skinny chested acting..... and many other kinds of chested acting as listed in Beerbom Tree's famous treatise on `chest acting through the ages.' But the guys sitting in front of us at the audition don't know that and don't have the time to ask us what kind of chest acting we specialise in.

It says in the script, man shaving in bathroom. Without saying a word they can see that I do `shaving in bathroom acting' Am I too fat, who knows, but at least they get to see bare flesh.... and this is important... it is not `acting' it really is bare flesh! I'm not suggesting that girls do this. it would be inappropriate and frightening, just as if I'd gone in with my face covered in Shaving foam.

I think I may have gone too far taking off my shirt. The rule might be.. go as far as you can but don't go so far that you can't travel on the tube looking like it! So according to the rule I went too far... BUT... I did have a towel I was able to throw over my shoulders.... so it wasn't so dumb. I got the job. In this game you have to sense how far to go. Too far and you look like a looney who would sing at the drop of a hat,

`I really need this job!!!'

Not far enough and you look like someone who has remained un-employed for years and are happy with it!

What's in the room?

All commercials castings are videoed these days. It helps them to remember and it is a screen test. Faces look different on screen against real life. And what they are looking for is the right face.

In the olden days they didn't video the castings, the process was too expensive. So they would have Polaroids, as they do today, but that was the primary means of recollection. I have sat through hours of auditions. The one thing they all have in common is that by 5.30 you have seen so many people that you wouldn't recognise your mother if she came in for a part.

I was thrilled to be the Associate Director, for a short while, on Bugsy Malone at Her Majesty's Theatre. We took over Olympia for a Sunday open audition and we saw 10,000 children. They had travelled from all over the country and all of them got to be seen by the MD's and Dance Captains and a few hundred got to be seen by Michael Dolenz, Gillian Gregory and me. When you've heard Charles Strouse's great song, `The Sun will Come up Tomorrow' sung a couple of hundred times, you begin to hope that it might not! How is any kid going to be spotted?

Later in the day when you are discussing re-calls, how do you recall any of them? Talented? Bright, Bubbly, young....? They were all of those things. Sometimes, it comes down to remembering, like in A Chorus Line, a certain coloured, distinctive leotard! It's the same for us.

During my fake glasses period I would always wear my bright apple green shirt. Unless I was being a business man. The shirt wasn't enough to stop the traffic in Regent's Street or have the people at the session comment upon it, but it was enough for them to say later,

`OK, which guy shall we have....

which do we remember....

there was that guy in the Green shirt?....

Oh, yeah, I made a note about that....

This is a slim theory for getting work but how many of the people at the session wrote on their notes,

'guy in the trousers and shirt... kind of muddy, brown grey colour, with no distinguishing features.'

At any kind of Casting... or Audition, wear something they will be able to make a quick note about. Hoping that they will remember it, is a long shot but they might make a note! The shirt is a way for them to remember you. It won't get you the job. Did I say, Don't dress up as a chicken?

Who is at the casting?

The Casting Director, she/he is your friend, they want you to be perfect, they want you to get the job. Really. They know only one of you will get the job, but they really want you to be right for it. That's what they do for a living! They got you there because they thought you were right for it. Confirm that they made the right decision by playing the game as close to the edge as you feel comfortable. This is the one person with whom you must have some kind of understanding.

This is one of the few people who maybe should know the truth, about your age. This is the one person who can put you up again for other things even if you don't get this one. This is the one person that you need to have a long term association with. Don't get me wrong, they do have a life! As I said before they are not looking for pen pals and they are not looking for obsequious chummy lovey huggy buddy lovers. It could be said that the closer you get to them being a friend the less likely they are to put you up for something. Because it gets too important, too nepotistic, too tense a subject. But they do want to know that you are a consummate professional with the occasional spark of genius and a twinkle in the eye. An actor who will always make them look like they made the right choice to bring you in.

Whilst I remember it, forget the spark of genius, that normally makes people late! Stick with the `you can always trust me' relationship. I'm not talking yet about real acting, I'm talking commercials.

Get the job, do the job, get paid.... or at worst...
Try to get the job, fail to get the job, and forget about it!

The other people in the room could be anyone. Try to listen to the names as they are introduced. I'm hopeless at this... I try to force my brain to listen to the names but.... If you do remember, then put them in your note book. Always have a note book that will still be with you in ten years! Get it to remember everyone you need to remember.

It's good to be able to say,
`Oh, yes, we met at the Kentucky Fried Chicken Shoot. What a lot of old nonsense that was!'
Oh, really? I directed that.
It was great wasn't it? I loved it. Fantastic. Super!
Golden Rule. Never be negative about anything!
Never.
What never?

Never. Nobody wants your opinion about anything. Life is too short. They are there to cast the commercial, not Vote for Worst Commercial of the Year or decide what was wrong with Pride and Prejudice, for which you weren't given an interview let alone given a part even though it's been your favourite book since you were seven.

The Director might be at the Casting. Try to catch his name. Ask your agent who will be there, she might know, put it in the book. We don't know what the director is looking for. But there are some things that we can be pretty sure they are not looking for. A chatter box who doesn't know when to end a sentence A Showbiz Kid who can't stop twinkling, unless that's what it says in the script.

An expert on Theatre, Movies, TV soaps, or the Industry in general. A Bon Viveur. (unless it says so) Anecdotes should only last 20 seconds and never be the start of `a turn.' Don't be someone who knows everyone or everything.... or actually anything!

Strangely enough, if they are experienced directors, they know that the best actors tend to be rather shy! Caution with all things though, don't play shy! They simply want to look at you and hear you talk. Talking to you mustn't be like pulling teeth or trying to shut the flood gates.

Be a normal polite human being.

The actor's job is to make the Director feel comfortable. They also know that if they choose you they may have to spend three days and nights in Mongolia with you! We all know some actors we would rather not do that with! Not many, but some.

The other people in the room could be from the Agency or the Client or the Youth Work Experience School Person. Treat them all to some friendly eye contact. Most of these people will look like they haven't noticed that you have entered the room and carry on sending E mails or Texting. It doesn't matter, the one person that requires eye contact.... is the camera! Most of the casting will be done later with the people who are too important to spend time at a casting. So it is the camera that will be telling them about you.

The Eyes have it! Look away and you'll look shifty. Look away and even though you are looking at the director, in real life, on tape you will look like you don't know why you are there! Answer questions to the camera. Talk to the camera. Smile at the camera. Focus on the camera. Ignore this if you feel this would inhibit your people skills, but be alert to the people and the camera.

We are hardly ever going to allowed to talk to the camera, unless we are presenting. But if you are doing stuff for the camera...like in the commercial casting... imagine that it is an old friend. Someone, with whom, you have a relationship. Your mother for example... just imagine that she is locked up in a nursing home watching you on tele... Ahh... so now you can be as relaxed as possible... it is not a machine!

My mother, is a wonderful woman but doesn't know what day of the week it is. You don't have to feel guilty about putting your mother in a home, it's the best possible place, once she has forgotten who you are and thinks that you killed all her children. Relax the time has come. Ask for help, Social Services really do care.

Years ago I did show for the BEEB called You Should Be So Lucky. It was universally hated by everyone except the viewers (we all say that about our shows) but it was true that it was the highest rated show the BBC ever screened at 4.30 on BBC 1 and at the time, the highest rated show they ever tried to hide on BBC 2 at any time slot! TFI Friday only ever picked up half of the viewing figures we had every Wednesday. It was a revelation to me, in terms of how focussed you need to be. The moment your eyes flit off camera, even for a milli-second, you lose contact with the audience.

More of this later but the real shock was.... who was I before they called `action' or in the case of Multi Camera Studio Work, who was I before they called `Cue Colin?' My face in repose was desperately miserable!

I should state categorically at this point that everything I say is what I believe to be true for me at this moment in time. You must decide for yourself if it's true about you. As a director, when you give a company notes at the end of the Dress rehearsal and you say, you, Charlie, must pick up the pace! Often all the actors assume that the note is directed at them! It might be, it might not be. Any notes I give you in this book are only for me.... I give them in the hope that some may help you to think through stuff you haven't thought about before and some you can say, 'Good, I'm glad he said that, it's obvious that the Prat is not referring to me! I am a much better actor.'

My face in repose is pulled down towards the lower depths. I had no idea I was such a miserable looking git. I'd often been told that, but to see it.... in those neutral moments between hearing the words, Turn over.... and Cue was horrifying. In the real world of TV these moments are yours, for your preparation and for the preparation of the technology. I'll speak about them in the appropriate chapter, they are important, if I remember.

But here in the Casting section they are important for another reason. The tape will be viewed by people you wont have met. It won't have been edited, they will fast forward between faces... between interviews... but they may also let the tape run during the `repose' sections. It's a tough one but keep your face working even when you are listening.

Golden Rule, most acting is listening.

What will they ask you? I don't know!
But we can take a pretty intelligent stab at what they will ask you. At the moment Arnie is being interviewed on all the Movie programmes on TV. I've seen at least three of these on different channels.

The questions are always the same, the answers are nearly always the same. He tries to make them funny and new but basically we could anticipate the questions and answers. Why don't we do the same at castings?

Because we are just actors answering questions, it has nothing to do with how good an actor we are.

That's true.

But then a casting is nothing to do with how good an actor you are either! Never mind the quality, feel the face? Remember this is not called an Audition it's called a Casting.

What's an audition?

That's where you normally show them how clever you are, at singing, dancing, acting, juggling. It is your job to convince them that you have the ability to do whatever they throw at you during rehearsals and then on the day, or day after day after day. It is a chance for you to impress them with your versatility. Your boundless energy, enthusiasm, dedication, etc. .etc..

Not much of any of that counts at a Casting.

The last thing they need to know is that you are versatile. Why would they want versatile? If they need a juggler, they'll get a juggler. If they need a lion tamer, they'll get a lion tamer. What they need is the person as outlined in the much debated script... they don't want someone to pretend to be the person in the much debated script. Golden Rule: They must never know that you are acting!

There is no God given truth here.... I know that I can't pretend to be a farmer. I know nothing about it. But at a casting recently it said in the script, close up of farmer's hands as he tests to see if an ear of corn is ready to harvest.

I don't know how to do this but I can imagine that you rub your hands together to separate the chaff and the wheat and then blow away the chaf.... and bite a few ears of corn.

I decided to play the `My hands are really rough' card.... my reply to a question, it didn't matter which, was that I'd just finished shovelling three tons of earth to build a new garage, so sorry, but my hands are in a terrible state!! They didn't check. If they had, they might have been able to spot that my hands are about as rough as a lovey actor's bottom. But they heard the words they wanted to hear.

In a perfect world they would prefer a perfect farmer, as it isn't, they are happy to get a rough handed actor!

What will they ask?

Your name, your agent, do you have any commercials running that conflict with this product? What have you been doing? What are you doing at the moment? What are you about to do? Have you read the script?

Can you think of any more? There may always be surprise questions that have come directly out of them reading your CV but basically that's it.

So why not have an answer ready? Something pithy, witty, simple, quick, intelligent, thoughtful, funny, normal, appropriate to the product but without mentioning it, that only lasts 10 seconds. Is this too much effort for 10,000?

It does sound a bit creepy. I know, but are we trying... or are we not bothered? Well, I don't want to look like I need the job too desperately. True, but you want to look like someone who'd really like to do the job.

Are you really meaning that I write the answers? No, I'm not asking that you be an automaton, who reels off set answers... but

They don't want to know that you have been unemployed for three months! But I have been.

Why haven't you been writing, researching, developing? No one can check up on these things! Obviously, you can't pretend to have been at The National for six months, if you haven't, but you mustn't sit at home waiting for the phone to ring! And if you have, don't tell them.

They will ask you these questions or something like it.... have an answer, that doesn't show off, but does put you into the right frame.

Never tell them you have prepared something! Just show them, as if it is you, if you can.

I recently went to one where the brief was `Peter Sellers, Pink Panther type person'

I used to be very funny on TV! I was almost noted for it... good! This will suit me fine and I already own a trench coat! I didn't have one of those turned down hats but I bought one for just 4.99 at a local fishing shop. The hat and the trench coat made me look just like Inspector C. I keep as much of this hidden in the waiting room. I'm certainly not going to show these actors that I've got the right hat in my pocket! They'd all want to borrow it! I'm not spending 4.99 on a hat I'll never wear so that they can get to spend three days in Paris!

But I broke my golden rule.... I asked if I should wear the hat. I should have just put it on without asking. They said, no better not, it will cast a shadow on you face. That's true but they only had to see me with the hat on for 10 seconds and that would have been enough to convince them. It would have been on tape regardless of the shadow. As it is the hat stayed in my pocket. And I didn't look that much like Peter Sellars. I don't regret the 4.99, you only get the jobs you are meant to get. And if you don't get any jobs... look for something else to do with your life. It's too short to fanny around not being an actor.

What will they ask you to do? Who knows?

They will ask you to do what it outlines in the script! I promise you that they will! The script might not look much. One page only. But contained within it's magic writing are all the clues to what they are looking for.

These are clever people but not in the way that we are clever. So if it says `Fat man slumps in front of TV' There is no point in going in your business suit looking skinny and hoping that on the spur of the moment they will decide to change the commercial to feature `A skinny man in business suit slumps in front of the TV.' What if I am skinny and have been told to wear my business suit?

First thing, make sure you are at the right address at the right time. There is always some kind of assistant there to hand you forms to fill in or Polaroids to take or keep the line moving. Ask them if this is the part for which you have been called and point out why you think it might be wrong. Their answer might be

Oh, not that's just a test script from the series, we are looking at you for the Business Man version.

Good, have you got a copy of that version script?
No, it'll be OK.
Good. Sit and think and never raise the subject again.
If she says,
Oh, sorry, today we are only looking for Fat Slobs. Then wait to be called, leave your jacket in the waiting room, take off your tie and shiny shoes, pull your shirt out and semi-slouch into the room. There is nothing else to do. There is no point in making an excuse, unless they ask why do you look like that? In which case they will know you have been given a bum steer.

Never be negative, never complain. It tells them more about you than you'd like them to know! No-one likes a whiner even if they are right. Some-one got it wrong. So what? You are either going to get the job or not! If you are negative...

They will always assume that you are complaining about them!

Golden Rule: In a dressing room after a show, or meeting a director at a cocktail party (huh, who am I kidding, when did I last go to a cocktail party!?) Never be negative!

The show was great, I loved it... I almost don't know why.... but it was much much better than you told me.... and you were terrific!

No, really! Oh, did that bit after interval go wrong? Well, you would never have guessed it!

We have a very strict family code. My sister is an Opera Singer, my nephew is an American Actor, my Nephew-in-law is an English Actor, My older son is an Actor, my younger son and my Wife are Directors....
The rule is... you are allowed to ask, after your show:
Who was best?
The answer must always be: You were!

Constructive criticism is only allowed to be dished out by the director or the Bastard Press! Family and friends and potential colleagues must always be in no doubt about `who's best!' You were!! You really were!! Life's too short! And it's too late to be a better actor.

Have you read the script? They might ask. Half of me might think the smart answer would be, if I said no, then the director will explain it to me, give me direction, and think I'm an intelligent thinking actor, who wants to know more. Wrong.

If you say no, then he assumes you were late, or so stupid that you didn't notice the pile of scripts displayed on the trendy smoked glass black IKEA coffee table. They will explain what they want but they will assume that you will have got a clue from the script.

What about learning the words? Most casting Directors would say that you don't have to. Fair enough. But what would an American actor do? British Actors are not very pushy or even very efficient at getting work. They believe that it is all luck. American actors/ business people/sports people need to try hard.

We British think that sending a team of 11 highly skilled, very highly paid players out onto the field to win, is based on luck!

Some of it is luck, but the harder you work the luckier you get! It's only two lines of text, learn it. You'd learn it if I offered to pay you 10,000. Why not learn it in the hope that I might!

You can still hold the paper as a security blanket but the camera needs to see your eyes! So if you do read it, hold it well below the camera eye line so that it can clearly see your face. That's what they are buying, what you look like!

Having done it, they may ask you to do it again. If they do, LISTEN to what they say.

It's extraordinary how many actors having been given a note, will then do another reading just like the first. The note normally wont be Stanislavskiesque, it will be slower, quieter, bigger, smaller, etc...they are not asking for you to repeat it just for fun.

Young Pathologist But They Are Not Looking For Experiments

Do I over-act, do I under-act? We are talking only about Commercial Castings now, remember.

Take one!: Over-act.

Take-Two!: Under-act.

Take three! Ask them.

This is your one shot, they are looking for all the things that real people look for in life: Love! Nice teeth, broad smiles, twinkly eyes, no subtext happy people to sell no subtext happy products!

We make some of the best commercials in the world, some are strange and obtuse, surreal and ethereal, poetic and cynical.... but mostly we are looking for nice people using nice products. If this conflicts with your radical pre-revolutionist anarchistic socialist anti-capitalistic values. Then Commercials are not for you!

As Jill Pearce would say: They are looking for Air Hostesses! Young Mothers in the real world are 13 years old. We can't allow this to permeate the world of Commercials where young mothers are 32! Think this through. There are jobs for people from the Ugly agency, plenty of them, far more here than there might be in the States, but mainly we need Air Hostesses to show us life at home with the kids. We have broken down a lot of the sexist stereotypes in life, but it doesn't necessarily sell more soap powder!

Over act? Are you sure? No, I'm not sure, but this is a one stop shop. You are either it, or you are not. You may be able to get a feel for the playing pitch from the way the script is worded, but not always. One person's over acting is another person's understated. If you have no clue which way to go then go the bright way! That could almost be another rule for life, couldn't it? (he said patronisingly with a knowing look in his eye and tilt of his old wise head)

Having done your two takes.... and they are just about to unceremoniously throw you out... you are allowed to play your, `Actually, could I give you just one last try, I think I've got it now,' card. and ask would they like it bigger, slower, louder, more Italian etc...?

Only do this as a last shot... they are trying to get rid of you... be aware that they have seen enough! They might not want to see any more because they have put you on the list! The time spent at the Casting is not proportional with the outcome of the choice! In fact it's more often you get the jobs you thought were lost and vice-versa.

I recently got a job for a Malt Whiskey in Scotland... the story is simple, A bloke walks miles and miles across Scottish moors and mountains on his way to the `Maturing Hall' where a blanket had slipped off a maturing keg of Macallens wonderful malt. ie: It is the best in the world (true, he agreed obsequiously) because it is looked after by very caring, very knowledgeable people. I would have thought, and so would you, that almost any card carrying member of Equity could have done this job. But they had seen hundreds of blokes. Why? Because they wanted what they wanted and they could afford to wait and find the one they wanted. When you rush around Sainsbury's you can afford to pick any packet of Kellogs Corn Flakes. Sainsbury's have accepted your challenge to make sure all those packets contain predictably controlled corn flakes of an understood quality. But you should just hold back before dumping any of the Avocados into the basket!

Incidentally, my mother said, when she knew what an avocado was, pick the avocados that just slightly give under firm pressure, with not too thick a skin! Very much like actors really!

At the Casting they will get you to do really silly stuff. In a room 12 by 10 containing a Casting Director, Director, Client, Camera and Camera Person, etc... they might ask you to walk across the Mountains of Scotland looking... looking at the mountains of Scotland... easy enough. Is it? It is as long as you are prepared to look a Prat. But that's why they hire actors... we are prepared to look like Prats! They are not asking you to act it out to look a Prat just for their Christmas Tape.

They want to imagine all the other ingredients and decide if we look like the person drawn in the Story Boards. They are not expecting us to be so brilliant that they can 'see' the snow capped peaks and 'feel' the clean chill wind rustling the fragrant heather that blows down to the mysterious loches that have for an eternity held the secrets of the Malt maker's art. If you were that good then you'd be in Hollywood with Liz Hurley making significant Austin Powers Movies. It's enough to look like a human being, looking.

They may ask you to eat something. They won't have anything there for you to eat but you will be expected to mime it. Just grit your teeth, smile and give yourself up to the moment! It won't hurt, it will soon be over and you might get the job. Commit yourself to the game, professionally! Don't hide your face, don't hold things up in front of your face, don't hold things so far out of frame that they 'lose' the mime. It is not a test of your improvisation or mime skills. On the day of the shoot, they will be able to afford to throw you more Kentucky Fried Chicken than you can shake a stick at but at the casting, be glad that you don't have to eat cold turkey out of a bucket.

They may ask for your profiles. Simply turn through 90 degrees, your whole body, one side and then the other. You would probably be standing. Sometimes they might say, show us your left profile. There is no answer to this, they don't really care which one you give them first, but it will always end up with a discussion about which one is the left and which one is the right. If they say Left.... you turn right, don't discuss it!

When you are doing profile acting don't try to hide your double chin by looking up at the ceiling or pull your stomach in to re-live the 60s. They may be looking for double chins and paunches. They will certainly notice that you are trying to hide them! They will then certainly ask for the Right profile.... which is when you'll turn Left! Best not to ask what they mean by....

Golden Rule never ask of anybody, What do you mean by.....?

Actors who ask questions, in the commercial casting arena are not considered, bright intelligent, thoughtful actors. They might be at the RSC. But at a casting they are considered dimwits who can't work out from the script what is required of them. If they can't work it out after 20 minutes of reading it in a waiting room, ten minutes of chat from an expensive Director is not going to help the actor `get it.' Got it? Good. I perhaps protest too much but I promise as a general rule. I speak with straight tongue and arched brow.

I'm not sure if I should help you with answers to the old `what have you been doing?' questions. Best to steer clear of the old jokes, like, `Do you mean this morning or for the last 40 years of my professional acting life?' But the general incontrovertible rule is that they are probably not listening to your answer and couldn't care less about your life, love, opinions, works or future. There are actors who seem to be able to pitch it absolutely right. A funny story, a relevant anecdote, a cute wink, a quick time step, a sophisticated observation about the Art of Motor Cycle Maintenance. And they have lots of friends in the business who occasionally give them work. But they still won't get it if they are not right for it!

Certainly, if you have the world from which to pick for your answer, (and you do) I'd try and tie it to the product without anyone knowing that's what you are doing!

I've watched hundreds of these interviews, there are no rules to getting it right.... but here are a few rules:

Never imply that you've been unemployed.

Always be bright and smiling.

Don't say the line too quickly.

Don't rattle it off.

Keep your eyes on the camera, or director if he is being the other actor.

This is your moment in front of the camera, no one else, revel in it. This next one sounds slightly tacky and I don't mean it in the context of a porn movie but.... the moment needs to be seduced. Notice I say the moment and not the Director or the Camera even, but there is an implicit secret between the person watching the played tape and you. An understanding.

Adopt a pro-active body posture. Sorry, that sounded like jargon! I mean of course lean forward. See notes later about depth of field.

Don't be a clever dick.

Don't have a subtext about, why am I here?

Why am I demeaning my talent, and training, for this? I promise you the camera will spot it!

Don't mumble. If you have a difficult name or your agent has a difficult name, really articulate it... so they have no doubt about who you are and where to contact you. I still say, on my mother's Christmas Cards, love from, your ever loving son, Colin Bennett, just in case! Mind you, even that clue is lost on my mother now!

Incidentally, it is surprising, I'm told, how many people write to Casting Directors with a photo and letter and then sign it with an unreadable squiggle! I hate that too.

Who are David and Lesley who keep sending us Christmas cards?

The jobs tend to go to those who are already working. Annoying isn't it? But you have to put yourself and your story into the working mind set.

Be a nice friendly ordinary person who is pleasant to work with. Be a caring person..... but don't care too much if you get it or not. Slow down at the strap line, where they might mention the name of the product.

Always slightly over sell the product. The clients are obsessed with their brands and won't notice that we think it's a joke to over articulate its name.

I recently did a job for PC World. The video they made featured an actor/ friend who visited a branch to buy a PC. In the story of the video 20 minutes later she left the store with a trolley bulging at the seams with add-ons, insurance, software, printers, scanners, piled high with expensive computer stuff... etc.. etc.. etc.. when I first saw it I laughed and clapped and turned to the PC World People, and with a smile, gave them a thumbs up at their joke.

It wasn't a joke. They sat in stoney silence looking at my as if I had gone off my head. They had not the slightest Idea why I thought it was funny. They want people to leave the stores with their trolleys piled high. They loved it, I loved it, loved it.
Why were you laughing?

No, I wasn't, I just thought it was really great. Wonderful. Hits the nail right on the head, no really, (shut up) Not laughing but just enjoying very loudly. (shut up) It's one of the best videos I've ever (shut and pretend to have a heart attack. Start choking and loosening your clothing) OK.

Never get the product name wrong. I once mistook Kleeneze for Kleenex... they never forgot it! And I wish I'd had some Kleenex with me.

Once, when working for Forte, I asked, who's Rocco?
It is amazing how instantly you realise that
you've opened your mouth just once too often.
The room suddenly goes cold and quiet.

Never let them know that we come from another planet.

Golden Rule: Always never quite say enough rather than say just that one line too far.

So let me summarise about Commercial Castings:

Get there early.

Dress and look appropriate or if in doubt like an airhostess. If you are looking very smart, take a big old jumper in a bag, just in case you need to knock the edges off it. and suddenly become a sailor!

If it's a branded food, why not buy some? When they ask you to mime.... here are my Mr Kipling's Battenburg slice almond square nibbly bits. Shall I eat one of those... you say out of the blue as if by magic rather than cynicism!

Shave! Or if in doubt be prepared to shave in the loo. Leave your coat in the waiting room! (keep your wallet on you) Don't make it look like you are just passing through on your way to somewhere more important.

Be patient. You will be kept waiting. So what? If you don't like being kept waiting find another more important job! Of course, if you can wait no longer, then, fair enough, go, with profuse apologies for not being able to wait.

Try and spot the Casting Director! Pretend you know them even if you don't. In fact, pretend to know everyone, even if you don't. Everyone in that building, from the person who might, on a slow day, offer you coffee (in your dreams) to the person who you think is the director must be greeted as a semi known colleague. That way you never un-knowingly look straight through, and ignore, or cut dead, Ridley Scott, if he's in the building. (which he isn't) But he might be and you might have worked with him years ago without knowing it and he has remembered you and you haven't got a clue who he is! (one breath)

That's an old trick we even used to Sell Electric Cookers, let alone the acting business. Always buy electrical goods from approved outlets, by the way. And never try to install it yourself unless you are foolhardy, which you probably are since you are an actor. And always switch the electricity off from the mains... unless you are in a hurry.

I may come back to commercials when I talk more specifically about 'being' in front of the camera but for the moment...

Let's try to get a job in The Bill. TV Drama! It's called. And it is!

It's not called a casting or an audition really, it's called a 'They'd like you to read for..... in The Bill' I use the word Bill generically. I also mean, any regular TV drama like a soap, or 'Casualty,' or 'Tired and Emotional Vets' or 'Idiosyncratically Lonely Policeman' or 'London's got a Cat up it's Tree.' etc...etc...

All the rules are now the other way round!

The Casting Director may only bring 3 or 4 people in to read for a part, some, very experienced, and single minded Casting Directors, may insist on only bringing in one! Then you have probably got the job. Though you could still lose it, if the Director doesn't like you.

If Commercial Casting is a little bit like pebble dashing a wall, (don't get me wrong the Casting Directors are still picking actors for their appropriateness) Casting a Drama is more like painting the window frames. It doesn't mean that Commercials are less important. They are more important. That 30 seconds will have cost the same price as an episode of Casualty. But the acting required for 30 seconds is not as sustained as it might have to be for 52 minutes.

At least they are looking for 'Actors!'

You might get a few sheets (sides as the Americans would say) of the script in the post, you might not, you might read it for the first time whilst you are waiting for your appointment. If you get it through the post, then why not learn it? You don't have to be DLP but you will be able to look up more frequently during the interview.

At least be familiar with it. But don't learn it in concrete. You won't have any idea of what else happens in the episode, everything that you do will be guessing.

One of my `Forensic Medical Examiners' in The Bill was quite a nice little part, which I did no better than competently, but I was horrified when I read the rest of the script to find that all the Policemen at Sun Hill thought I should have retired years ago! I didn't know that! I was being a young vibrant middle-aged person. It is always about how others see you. One very elderly lady actor, she would prefer the word actress, who was 83 years old, said that she could never play Grandmothers because she had never even been married or had children! Presumably, that was still to come! She thought of herself as the young woman she had always been, once.

Ahh,.... sorry I've just gone a bit sad.

You have got the appointment. Be there early, you might get out early, be there to read the script and have the coffee that you will be offered! (at last) Wear the right clothes, but remember they would be horrified if you came as a chicken or a judge, they are expecting `actors' so the game must still be played but played at a much higher level. Actors do tend to be very, very casually dressed and so too will the Director. So if you do too much they will wonder if you are a `real' actor. But the Casting Director will want you to dress as appropriately as you can. Because they want you to get the job.

We are all capable of wearing a suit, but does it look part of you... or does it look like the average best man at a wedding who has been dragged out of his Kwickfit Overalls to wear a morning suit and hat, desperate for the moment half way through the evening when, having tied a cat to the wedding car, thrown up in the formal gardens, can relax, undo the collar and wander around looking for the one pretty bridesmaid.

The chat before the reading is still irrelevant, it is still to see if you can talk without moving your eye brows, to hear if you can talk without loud acting and voice enunciation. To get a feeling for what kind of Forensic Medical Examiner you would be if you were one! It might still help them to say that you once used to work in a

Mortuary, or Market Garden, or Local Newspaper, or appropriate employment, when you were young. But they mustn't spot that you have planted it into the conversation!!! Same rules about being nice, not talking too much, not knowing anything.

But you are allowed to ask about the part. You are not allowed to tell them how you think the part should be. They will tell you all you need to know and will direct you, so you are allowed to respond in the way any actor would in a semi-rehearsal way, but know when to stop. I'll talk about behaviour on set later in more detail but this is getting close to the process so I'll touch on a few things about the Director. He will have thought it all through already.

You are probably having this meeting just seven days away from actually shooting it. So he will probably have already done most of his pre production. In other words he will know when he is shooting your scene, where he is shooting it, what furniture is in the room, what shots he will use, how it might be lit and a hundred other considerations made. He did all this without even knowing that it would be you playing the Reporter, Nurse, Witness, Crook etc.

The last thing he is looking for is a precociously intelligent actor who will contribute wonderful ideas to make the 50 minutes of TV better than he ever expected! What he is looking for is someone who fits whatever part the writer suggested and when told to stand on 'that mark,' won't move around. I exaggerate slightly, he is looking for an actor! He has a camera person, a sound person, a continuity person... they all know what jobs to do. He will expect the same of you. You are another fully trained professional who knows what their job entails. It doesn't entail directing, re-writing the script, or coming up with great ideas!

He asks you to read the part, he may play all the other parts, especially if he used to be an actor, (though not many were) or he'll get the Casting Director to read the other parts. Unlike the Commercial where they are looking for the finished work on the first reading, here, at a sensible drama audition.... they are looking for the finished work on the first reading! Best to read that again! They are looking for someone that they wont have to 'work hard with' to get them up to speed.

Believe me this is as close as you will get to being Directed. You may never talk to the Director again.

Golden Rule:

> Take one!: Underplay, but be positive.
> Take two!: Do less.
> But be certain about who you are.

Here's a list of rules, about sight reading, you can break if you want to:

Give very positive eye focus to the other reader.

Read a line ahead, then look up and deliver the line.

Take your time,

Keep it quiet.

Make them drag `a performance' out of you. (only half true)

This is not Pantoland. Coronation Street is slightly different, they do tend to like, `turns.'

Don't PLAY any jokes that you spot in the script.

Don't `do moves' around the room.

Don't do gestures.

Be still.

Don't look like you've learnt it too solidly. Don't worry about mistakes, pretend to be flexible!

This is about people, there probably won't be a camera present, so this is about making the Director feel that you are a safe pair of hands. A nice person who knows when to shut up, learn the lines and not bump into the furniture.

Does it go without saying that if there were a camera in the room, it should be ignored in this circumstance!? Then I'll say it... Ignore this camera!

As they are about to throw you out with a polite thank you, you can still play the `May I have another go' card. But be certain that you haven't already out stayed your welcome.

You get the phone call, you got it! Great! The money won't be much more than you get working part time at the Double Glazing Telesales Office but what the heck, it's real acting!

What next?

The Production Office phone with the next few pivotal dates, the read through, and a range of days, two or three of which will be the shoot days. In the case of The Bill they will tell you which colour team you are playing for. This is vital information other wise you'll end up in the Actor's Nightmare, wrong place, wrong time, wrong script, wrong part. Each episode of a long running series is normally given over to various completely separate teams. Each with their own, script, actors, story, locations, Casting Directors, etc...

The Wardrobe Supervisor will phone for a fitting day. This might well be the read through day. They still call it a read through but an actual read through is very remote. Who needs it? No-one. It's too late to re-write it.

You will be sent a script. This may be in several different colours, relating to the various versions in re-writes, up to that point. Learn the lines! Learn them really well.

You will also be sent a Contacts Sheet! It will probably be the first page of the script. Note the name of the Casting Director,

The Director, The Producer, the Wardrobe Supervisor and the Various Floor Managers or First Assistants. You'll meet them all (apart from the casting director who is now long gone) and you might as well know their names. Put them in your book. And then put this sheet in a safe place where you will be able to find it in ten years time.

You will also be sent a separate document with times of crew calls and locations and actors call times. Go through it as soon as you get it and check to see that it all makes sense and that you are free for the moments that they call you.

It is important that you get this stuff at least three days before your calls. But you don't need it a week before your calls. TV companies are very efficient at sending these details so don't panic, they will call you and make contact. Only panic if you thought your first call was the day after tomorrow and you have heard nothing. If you have one, get your agent to ring. But don't ever try to chase this information up too early!

In TV you can only do one thing at a time. And the people you will be working with next week are busy this week doing the previous green team episode. You may complicate the system by bugging them too soon.

I'll write though the whole process. Not because you need to know it, though I might think of something useful to give on the way but simply because you might think you should know something. It's a very sophisticated routine, where nothing is left to chance and as long as you follow the path that they lay out before you, even an actor can't get it wrong.

Wear clean underwear for the costume fitting, a clean shirt, clean socks and easily removed shoes. Sounds obvious doesn't it? If you go in shorts, tee shirt and bare feet sandals, they will have to find a proper clean shirt, socks, and all that goes with it, then clean it again after you have worn it for the 30 seconds of the fitting. When all they really needed to do was throw a jacket on you and say, that's fine! They won't mind but most actors would hate to have to wash someone else's clothes!

This is the beginning, the first of my really serious acting notes. Let's look at what they have put you in. A pathologist Suit, pathologist tie, pathologist shirt, shoes and socks. These are really boring pieces of clothing. Boring, really boring. In the script it said, Slightly Eccentric Pathologist. So in my mind I saw a coloured bow tie and perhaps even a coloured waistcoat, perhaps a flamboyant shirt or (heaven forbid) Suede Shoes! But no, it is boring.

SPOT THE DIFFERENCE

THEATRE TIE!

TV TIE

AND YET IT'S THE SAME ACTOR

They pick the most boring ties they have, put one of them on me and then send me off to show the director with two or three other boring ties as a choice.

No, says the director. Let's see some more ties... I think, Oh, good I'll get a coloured bow tie this time... But no.... they look for ones even more boring. That's the one, he says when he sees the one that I can hardly see, even though I'm wearing it!

Why is this an acting point?

There are at least three things to say about it.

The most significant point I'll save for when I'm really talking about `real' acting. This is too crucial a note to hurry here at a costume fitting.

The other two notes are:

However good an actor I am,

will I ever be as much like a Pathologist...as the tie is like a tie?

In an acting competition between me and the tie. The tie would win! Everyone would agree that it looks like, sounds like, moves like, behaves like, eats and drinks like ... a real tie! Not everyone, however, good as I try to be, would agree that I look like, sound like, move like, behave like, eat or drink like... a real Pathologist.

What the director is tacitly saying to me is that he wants ME to be as convincing a pathologist as the tie is being doing ITS job! The second technical reason is that in Black and White movies there is a uniformity in the grey scales... hopefully nothing hits `peak white' and nothing hits `crushed blacks.' In colour TV it is very easy to hit the colours that are either going, at worse, `to bleed' or at least pull the eye and distract it. It is just as easy for a tie to over act as it is for an actor.

We don't want to call him `The Pathologist with the tie.'

This book, with the right dust cover, could be very convincing as The New Testament and Psalms, with an introduction by the very reverend What's his Name? I doubt if I could. I aspire to being that good.

I'll touch on the third reason just to give you time to think about it....

I am eccentric. So I don't need to play eccentric. Neither does my tie.

I don't tell you that I am eccentric just to impress you. In fact, I don't think that I am eccentric. But if I were to say, to my family, 'I don't think I AM eccentric!' They would all fall off their chairs and say, Yeah, right! In the same way: Would I need to play the fact that this Pathologist is a man and not a woman? If I were to `PLAY' being a man.... the camera wouldn't know what to think about the sexual preferences of the pathologist!

So, the tie is fine!

The next time I meet any of these people I will be a Pathologist and they will be far too busy to talk to me. So, if you really feel the need to talk to any of them, do it now!

Just as a warm glow travels through your body as you enter a new Stage Door in a Theatre miles from your home, where there is a Dressing Room with your name on the door, so too, it is very pleasing that as you arrive for your first call, someone will be expecting you and know where you need to go! Someone wearing a baseball cap back to front, a clip board and Walky-Talky will already seem to know your name and why you are there and will point you towards an endless supply of coffee, tea and bacon sandwiches.

Life doesn't get much better than this!

Try to catch his/her name, you'll see them again when they point you to a room or caravan or recreational vehicle where your costume has already made itself at home.

If you haven't already done so, separate the pages of your script that are relevant to today's shoot schedule, and forget the rest. Find a pocket in your costume where your script can live without anyone else knowing! You will be glad not to fill your pockets with the full script, for which three trees have been sacrificed. And yet you might just like a reminder of what to say in scene 7. Word of warning, it might say, on the schedule, that they are only doing the location 3 scenes. Learn all your scenes. The schedule is law! But there are sometimes reasons for changing it.

For example, in one of my scenes, I was examining a dead body. We had to re-schedule because the woman who was playing dead wasn't feeling well enough and had to be sent home! So someone else's scene was brought forward from tomorrow. It is truly embarrassing if you haven't got a clue about the words. You might have a great excuse about why you don't know them but.... who cares?

Another trap waiting for you to fall in is the alternate scenes schedule. You are in Scenes 1, 3 and 5, (in the same room) and perhaps a final boring-tie-loose-ends-up scene 32. The real expense of TV work is moving the camera. Shooting with the camera is not as expensive as moving it from here to there, to look at these people rather than those people. So don't assume that there will be any kind of break between shooting scenes 1 and 3. You might have thought you could use the time to brush up your words. Chances are they will shoot them, consecutively 1,3,5,18, 32.

Luckily these words are easy enough to learn, in short sentences, without any reference to iambic pentameter, but you don't want to learn them in public with a camera looking at you.

You may find yourself in a caravan with other actors from the same scene, feel free to ask them if they'd like to have a rattle through the lines. Most of them will want to.... apart from the regular players who might prefer to seem so unconcerned that they don't need to learn them. They do need to learn them and they are happy enough to have quick spin through them. But they won't be happy about you needing them to help you learn lines. Two or three times through should be enough, then they'll lose interest.

 Don't forget everyone is there to do their own job. You, to be a nervous visitor and them to be a cool regular. When you are a cool regular then your grasp of the verbatim words won't be so important either.

Do you have a prop to use? Doctor's stuff, Oxy Cutters, Small Arms Gun Cleaning? In the theatre we wouldn't think twice about the ASM getting some rehearsal props for week two. In TV unless you ask, you won't see your Gun until the moment you are standing on the mark ready to go.

Then the director will say:

OK, this is where you clean the gun, don't forget you have been a professional soldier for twenty years!

Ooops.

The props man or armourer might have looked for you and shown you how to do it, but he might have been busy all morning setting explosions and trying not to kill people. When he sees you in your combat uniform, green and black stripes all over your face, he is going to think, just like the audience, that you know exactly how to disassemble a Kamakasi 33/45B Auto Load, Repeat Burst, Impact Function Gun Thingy.

It is your job to seek him out and ask him for some practice.

I've picked the worse case scenario but any prop can be a nightmare without time to think about it.

I once had to give evidence in a court. As I stood for the very first time on the mark, a props man handed me a note book and sheaf of papers, on which I had my evidence.

Great, you might think! Trouble is, this is a very good caring props person.

He hasn't just photocopied the script onto the evidence. He has written out the evidence in what might have been the 'original' form.... ie: I was proceeding along Gower Street in a southerly direction.....

In the real scene the Prosecutor asks me,: We know already that you were in Gower Street and moving in a southerly direction, what exactly did you see outside number 62? Erm....

You do know the words.... but you know the 'real' words from the script, whilst having to look down at a paper that contains some similar but not quite exactly the same words.

Far from being an Aide memoir it is a Mal d'Bottom. If you had seen this prop earlier you could have scribbled the 'real' words in the margin of the evidence and it could the have been some help to you, if you had suddenly dried. We can't expect a Prop person to know that he wasn't helping us. Everyone has their own job.

Meanwhile, we haven't got that far. We have been to make up where they fiddled slightly, we have been seen by the wardrobe supervisor and given an OK, and we have found the prop person and seen the bit of paper, Stethoscope, Bren Gun, Car, Van or what ever other prop they've picked for us. We've rattled through the lines, no acting, just words, with the available actors and drunk three gallons of coffee, swapped anecdotes of nights in the theatre and wondered if they really will get around to us.... what shall we do now?

Make sure you know your scene for tomorrow as well! This is a very predictable business but they may suddenly say to themselves that if we rattle all his scenes off today we may not need to call him in again tomorrow! You may not have worked for three years and would be more than glad to drag the job into two days. Two days of eating properly, gallons of free coffee, more theatrical anecdotes than you can shake a slapstick at, but no, they would rather get rid of you. So at 25 past 5 they suddenly say let's just do that little bit with the pathologist at the car! Oh, bum!

I was the keeper of Deep Thought in The Hitch Hiker's Guide to the Galaxy. I was called on the Wednesday morning at 5 am to have the alien head gear built onto me. Once strapped into it, I couldn't eat, talk, laugh, drink, walk, sit, stand, think, pee or go anywhere. Great a chance to learn the 1 minute 50 second speech. A monologue about the arrival of the answer to the secret of life, I think.

Occasionally, someone would bring me a cold tea to drink through a straw from a plastic cup and tell me that they might not be ready for me that day. This was the old Ealing Film Studios where at 5.30

the plug was pulled out of the wall by the electricians, regardless of what was in front of the camera. These people thought they had jobs for life, so we were meant to just be grateful that they had graced us with their presence.

It's all a bit different now. But in those days the plug was pulled by a man in his overcoat ready to go home with a stop watch in his hand! By the end of Wednesday the plug was pulled and I hadn't stood in the light. So off with the disguise and another call for 5 am tomorrow. This happened three days in a row. No-one minds. I didn't mind. Glad to be working. Incidentally, never complain! Never, never, never complain. I know I've said it before but... never.

So, another day in which to practice the words, sit in a cupboard, get hungry and wait.... for 5.30 to be sent home again. We now arrive at 5 o'clock on the Friday evening, this is the last filmed shoot day of the series! If we don't film it today, it may never be filmed at all. They won't use me now will they? I ask. They might, they might, don't go!

Meanwhile, I mutter the words, in the desperate wish that I had learnt them just fractionally better than I had. After all I had assumed that I would be given a chance to practice them at least once by the time the camera turned over. 5.15pm. I doubt if they will get to me now will they? Just lean there, don't fall over, don't move, they might. 5.25. The man in the overcoat and Tupperware lunch box has begun to hover around the plug, whilst his chums line up at the clocking out point and everyone is shouting on set.....'Call the Keeper of Deep Thought, ...the Keeper of Deep Thought.... Deep Thought..... the Keeper of Deep...'

The young chap in the backwards baseball cap drags me, tripping and skipping along corridors towards the black void with the over-lit centre that is a TV studio.

`Up the ladder' shouts the well known and great TV director. What ladder? Find a ladder! The cameraperson several miles away on a giant crane calls out, `Where is this scene taking place?'
Up a ladder!

What ladder, What for, why?

It's 5.27...; we have three minutes left!

`Action! calls the director.

What am I supposed to be looking at? calls the cameraperson.

The man trying to climb the ladder.

5.28. I am now standing on the very top most unsupported step of a giant A frame step ladder. I am suddenly blinded by an electrician finding me with a lamp, the crane looms over other bits of the set and settles... OK shouts the camera person.
5.28'.30" `Action'

I speak the speech flittingly on the tongue, without gestures or pauses, without fluffs , hesitations, repetitions, deviations, 1 minute 30 seconds and as I reach the last word..... I, and the rest of the known Universe is plunged into matt black science fiction bible bobbing oblivion.

Almost instantly people are coiling cables and saying goodnight and going home as I stand waiting to be rescued at the top of a ladder. It was a nightmare.... but I did know the words (more or less, I think) and got them in before the light went out. Acting it wasn't, It was not included in the final show and I was given the Prophet Zarquon, as a consolation prize, who, ironically only just arrives in time for the End of the Universe!

I did a series for the BBC many years ago called The Songwriters and we were making the episode about Ivor Novello.... the largest Sound stage in Europe had orchestra, settings, hundreds of dancers being Ruritanian Soldiers etc... Princesses, Kings, Queens, Peasants etc.... And it was 10 o'clock at night. The rules were slightly more flexible at Television Centre and you could run over the recording slot, with the agreement of the people who had regular jobs, for a maximum of 15 minutes, subject to negotiation. So it was agreed to finish at 10.15 pm.

The time was very quickly ticking away with the one big take yet to be recorded.... Turn over... The Director, called out to make one last change.... the Floor manager shouted back.....

`There's no time to get it right!...... there's only time to do it!'

I still feel guilty that I wasn't able to be better.

It is not quite so tough to do things on time nowadays since no one has regular jobs and they all want to work, so are more co-operative, and more flexible.

Let me go back a step.... to your visit to the makeup department. Be careful before you let them touch you hair! Never quote me on this OK? IT'S A SECRET. They are employed to fiddle with you hair, so that's what they'll do... but is it what you were expecting? Will the director recognise you next time he meets you on the floor. Just think about how often you have hated your hair having come straight out of the hairdressers.... but this time you are not going to be given the chance to go home and wash it into another shape... you are going straight onto the set to try and be the person you thought you were meant to be... but now you look like someone else's idea of what you are meant to be! Just be careful!

Girls are sometimes allowed to do their own hair and the best make up people will be very careful to do what you want, but just keep an eye on them. This is particularly important if you have too much hair, like I used to have... it was always better either left un-combed or I did it myself. If combed it could only look like a large haired bouffanted quiz show host. And once combed it would never go back to looking normal again for the rest of the day.

Hair is a terrible thing! All too often on TV you see great or at least competent acting being done by someone whose hair is over acting! This is particularly true of Americans and Grey hair. It is as if the actor, so terrified that people will think that he/she really is grey has said to the hair department, make it look false! The hair should look as much like real hair as the tie looked like a tie.

I can never understand why even in great movies... say Batman Returns... where they have spent millions of pounds on effects... why it is necessary for the great leading actor to look like he has stuck on a joke shop moustache. Indeed, it looks like he stuck it on himself!! This stuck on moustache would not even be good enough for The Mikado!

Why did they have such stiff hair in the windy ranch in Dallas? Well, I guess because it was so windy.... their problem is to re-create it in the interiors in a studio. By making the hair predictable they could re-create the hair predictably.

Continuity is everything. If it is going to take three days to record one scene as it often does in a 'shot on film' drama. They need to be able to reproduce that hair each time. It helps if you have thought that through for yourself, don't let them have to worry about it or they might do something drastic.....

The really difficult things to get continuity on are dirt, blood, sweat and general broken down stains. The classic examples are big disaster movies. You know these are not cheap movies, they are destroying millions of dollars worth of Fire engines, helicopters, skyscrapers and yet they really do have trouble keeping the hero's appreciably deteriorating vest in continuity. Suddenly it gets better for one shot.... It's almost impossible to stop the bruise or blood stain from moving around his/her face.

All these problems are someone else's but it is incumbent upon you to help the process along.

Don't ever volunteer anything that you might find difficult to reproduce.... drinking, smoking, gesturing.

Great! a chance to have dirty secret cigarette without feeling guilty. I haven't smoked for 30 years but I secretly wouldn't mind having the odd one!

They, and you, know that you may be called upon to reproduce this action maybe twenty times. Do you really remember when you took a puff from the cigarette?, When you took a dramatic swig from the gin or waved your hand in the air. They will EXPECT you to have remembered when you did it and will EXPECT you to do it, the same time and time again. Suddenly, just for the sake of wanting to eat a bit of free cake the scene has become, for you, a scene about remembering when you last took a chunk! Let's just run through why this is so important!

What actors don't know is that the directors, when they come to edit the whole thing together, are not looking for the `best' take, ie: The one that is perfect in every way, dramatically, emotionally, chemically.

They would like that it to be the one they chose but... In the one where all those things were happening absolutely correctly, the cigarette was too long, the glass was in the wrong hand, the vest was too clean, the mouthful of cake was too full. And at the end of the day, or edit, it is better to choose the take where the continuity was right even if the acting was suspect! We all spot bad continuity but who knows what suspect acting is?

There are always exceptions but in general the order of events is this:

First we take a `wide master' The whole scene from entry to exit shot with a wide lens so that everything is seen. This is for safety. We might cut to this version in at the top of a scene, just to establish who is in the room and where they all are in relationship to each other.

We might rehearse this on tape. If the director feels that his `talent' as the Americans call it are always best on their first go, (which most actors are) then he might record this rehearsal just in case something magical happens. It rarely does since no one except the actors know what is about to happen, and even THEY have never seen the room or the set or have practised it standing up on the marks!

So it might be the best performance, but the boom gets into shot, or the actors throw shadows over each other, or we can hear traffic noise or a million other things. None of these things are ever the actors fault. This is always true.

It is vital that you know you are about to do endless takes. It is vital that you never get paranoid. Everyone else on the set thinks that you will get better and better by doing more takes.... they are not actors and don't know that in fact you are getting worse and worse, more and more tense, more and more paranoid, more and more unsure of what you need to do! Believe me, it is not your fault. I guess it might be if you can't get further than the first line without drying, but mainly if you are remembering the words, then you are getting it more or less right. They are looking for other things that make them do more takes than required.

In commercials all those takes are just to impress the client about how difficult making little masterpieces is. When they see the invoice they will know why it cost so much. They want to spend the money. They believe that by spending that kind of money they are paying the God of Mamon his dues and are bound to be successful in selling the soap powder. In fact, of course, it is easy and I don't think I have ever seen a commercial that I couldn't have made for between 8,000 to 20,000. That's not the point! Most commercials cost between 60,000 to 250,000 to make. This is to pay for the Emperor's Clothes!

Never, never, assume that it is your fault that it is taking 36 takes to do a very simple sequence. You are a very small part of the jigsaw, just relax, enjoy, and do what you are told.

So we have the wide master! Good, now if World War three breaks out we could still walk away from the location having done nearly enough. But now we must go in for some tighter shots.

We need to see faces, body language, tears etc... So having got the wide we need a mid two shot, showing the main speakers, though neither of them in close up. This again is for safety. Everything is for safety because it costs so much more to come back another day! Also we need to tell the story clearly. A part of that story is... who is talking to whom... and where are they in the room and how they react to each other. Remember, unless told other wise, it is vital that you reproduce in your mid and close up shots what you did in the wide shot.

Now we will do the Reverses. These might still not be very close up but will positively feature one speaker. The other speaker might be fringeing the shot, out of focus on the edge of the frame. In other words we might be looking over the shoulder of the listener. It looks good and it ensures that we still know where everyone is in the room. The eye loves to see out-of-focus foreground, it seems to sharpen up the main speaker and tells us slightly more about the world in which they are living. So even if the foreground were not the listener it might be a potted palm or coffee cup or other room dressing. Mind you if there is too much of this then you know the director has lost the plot and is just being a bit arty. He is allowed to be.... never express and opinion, either to him or to anyone!

As the BBC always used to say, `You are never alone with a microphone.' Some one will hear you, just when you thought you were being clever or smart, you'll turn around to find the trendy young poser standing right behind you.

[Cartoon: Two figures facing each other under a boom microphone. Caption reads "You ARE NEVER ALONE – WITH A MICROPHONE". Thought/speech bubbles include "BASTARD DIRECTOR!", "STUPID WRITER!", "I HATE WHAT SHE'S DONE TO MY HAIR!", "BL**DY PRODUCER!", "DEAF SOUNDMAN!"]

Having said that, I don't know ANY directors you could say that about!

Now we might be ready to go in for the close up. Normally, we might get the actor with the most difficult task to go last. If they need to cry or emote their close ups would come after everything else. They can get a chance to tune in to the event. Don't blow all your tears into an uncontrollable heap on the wide master... because you still have a long way to go.... you might be all cried out by the time we need to see one single tear dribbling down your damask cheek.

Some directors might want tears from take one... but in normal workaday TV, life is too difficult to get it right twenty times in a row.

So we now have the wide master, the mid two shots and our close ups.... now we need the other speaker's REVERSES. Now it starts to get difficult.... because we need to move the camera.... remember that's the costly difficult bit. We might need to re-light, move the sound department, move furniture, move the actors to positions where they can no longer see the other speaker. Half the crew might go and have a cup of tea, whilst all this is going on, but they might prefer the actors to stay where they are, on their marks, either old marks or new marks. You must stay where you are put unless told otherwise.

You may not think that anything is happening, so you sidle off your mark to chat to the other actor... don't, someone somewhere is trying to balance the colour on your face, or whatever.

So now it's time for your reverses. You are told to speak to this bit of Gaffer tape hanging from a stand, even though you can see the real person to whom you should be speaking. It's tough but you have to `pretend,' They will give you an `EYELINE' to talk to. Just grit your teeth and do it. It is very easy to OVER ACT when talking to a prop person's hand. Just hang on to Stanislavski, try to remember what it was like to talk to a real person.

Incidentally, if you were doing reverses with Brando, you might never get to meet him! He would do his reverses on your day off and you would do your reverses once he had left the building. Just let it go, be glad you are working with.... just be glad you are working.

In theatre we love to overlap lines, it adds pace and excitement, energy and spontaneity in TV and film we mustn't, unless told otherwise, step on each other's cues! It is the director who will give it pace and sew it all together. He won't be able to do that it if your lines can be heard overlapping the other speaker's lines on the other speaker's reverses. So it is important that the actor who is out of shot, doesn't act too boldly, loudly or quickly. If you are not sure, you are allowed to ask, `Am I in this shot?' And they may say, `No, we are just doing Marlon's reverses.'

It is always best to look around to see where the camera is pointed before asking this question or they may think you are slightly daft. There are occasions where the camera is pointed in your direction but the shot is so TIGHT that you are there to give the speaker an eyeline or to throw in the odd line or two of your own.

We have now moved the camera a couple of times, and you have managed to get through your bits without making any mistakes, if fact, hopefully you might even have been getting better at the actual acting, and you might have managed to cry a tear or two. I'll speak about this later.

But now someone says, `Are you sure we haven't CROSSED THE LINE?'

SAY NOTHING!

Crossing the Line is a little bit like the off side rule in football. You can describe technically what the rule states but whether you have broken the rule depends on where you were seeing the infringement from and whose side are you supporting. In almost every production, a few moments will be spent discussing Crossing the Line. Say Nothing.

The rule is this: The Line, for acting, is drawn between the two noses of the talking actors and extends into infinity in both directions. The camera must stay either on this side of the line or on the other side of the line but must never cross it! Sounds simple enough? It's not simple once you start moving the camera and the actors for subsequent shots in the same scene.

Imagine two actors talking nose to nose, face to face for the whole scene. We take a wide shot and Charlize is on the left of frame and Mr Bennett is on the right. We take reverses. We can't see Bennett but we know he is to the right of the picture, Charlize is to the left of frame looking right, we give her some LOOKING SPACE on the right of the frame to make a better balanced picture and to confirm that Bennett hasn't moved. Now we take Bennett's reverses, we don't cross the (imaginary) line, we turn the camera to point at him. He is looking left. All is well.

If we had crossed the line, they would now look like they are now standing side by side instead of looking at each other. Two people talking to each other need to continue to face each other, not be both looking from left to right, in the same direction.

In the attached photo, Charlize, one of the finest actors of her generation, is pleading with me... I am saying, 'Charlie, I'm a married man, get over it!' In the bottom pictures it looks like we are saying these words to some third party.

If we had been sitting on a bench side by side then it really wouldn't matter where we shot the scene from because the bench would be our predictable point of geographical reference.

Though I would still be saying, 'Charlize pull yourself together... if only we had met years ago.'

The rule doesn't always apply if the camera work is very fluid, ON THE SHOULDER, as long as the audience has been able to keep aware of where everyone is placed.

More complicated versions of this happen all the time. We are on the kerb, a car pulls up and someone leaves the car and enters the building. Bear in mind that the viewer is not seeing real life, they are seeing a sequence of shots recorded possibly over several days. Each part of which took at least one hour to set up and shoot.

Car arrives from the right, man exits car and leaves into the building crossing the sidewalk left. If we accidentally cross the line that connects the door of the building to the car door, the man will suddenly be crossing the pavement from left to right! Is he going in or coming out? Goodness this is about as boring to describe as the Off side rule and can be argued over by everyone except the actor. If they lose the plot so badly that they accidentally ask the actor for his opinion, (which they will never do) simply say, `Sorry, that's a difficult one, I'm not sure.' Even if you are absolutely sure that you know the answer, just leave it!

You can tell that I'm getting tense. I made the mistake and I still regret it!

Years ago I made an ad where a father plays with a train set in an attic whilst his son, with the help of Yellow pages, buys a signal box. `Oh, Hello Ben,' says the father, that line took 39 takes, incidentally. After take 23 I thought I was talking in Chinese, `Ahhm, Harlung bin.'

Just to prevent you going insane it is worth remembering that they are looking for perfection. and they have the time to wait for it.... don't try to do 39 different versions of `Oh, Hello Ben.' simply stay focussed and change it as they direct you but otherwise simply hang on to the simple greeting to a boy whose head is no longer coming up through a hole in the floor and who went home three hours earlier.

Ten years goes past and they are still bombarded with complaints saying that the father didn't say....'Oh, Hello Ben' .....and then `Oh, Thank you, Ben!'

So......... They set it up again. New set, different studio, different director, different everything except the father, me. Strangely, the pullover I was wearing in the original commercial was my own. It still lurked up in the attic where we keep all our old flares, platforms and tank tops. I took it with me for the shoot.... They preferred the one they had bought, to match the old one, rather than the original, still in mint condition. I no longer wear pullovers! Think about that, even the pullover wasn't able to re-create his previous performance.

Neither was my hair! Now it is grey, then it was..... well it wasn't dark... but it appeared to be dark. So they darkened my hair... I now looked more like Ronald Regan, with the dark bottle of Grecian 2000. And was called to the set. They started setting up the shot, the final shot of the commercial, where the father now says to the boy he hasn't seen for many years, and who is now married with three kids of his own, `Oh, thank you, Ben!'

We are about to do take one and I should have kept my mouth shut, simply waiting to deliver the immortal and new words but.... I said, `Are you sure we're not Crossing the Line?' They looked at me as if I had said, `Your Mother was the Child Bride of a Camel.'

They smiled and showed me the playback of the previous version.....

`There, you see, you are looking from left to right!...... we cut away to the `PACK SHOT and when we return you.... are.... Oh.... looking from..... shit..... right to left!

Sorry guys, we have crossed the line! Move everything!'

We then shot it.... all done in about an hour, 300 or so takes.

Trouble is.... I was right, dead right, and my case was strong,
                 but was just as dead as if I'd been wrong.

If you ever see the commercial... it MIGHT have looked better if we had shot it from the other side of the line!

Anyone reading this who was involved with that previous production, please accept my most humble apologies for ever saying anything other than, `Oh. Thank you, Ben!'

Say Nothing, never talk to the director, never even stand in the coffee queue with him, just in case you are tempted to say, `I really like working with you, I do hope we get a chance to work together again soon.'

I promise, if you ever hear yourself say that, then you will see a kind of shutter coming down over his eyes and he will wander away aimlessly looking for a toilet to drink his coffee in, in peace.

A director is responsible for getting the product made on the shop floor. He is worried about the time, the light, the crew, the actors, the wardrobe, the schedule, the rain, the traffic, the blocking, the shots, the story.

The producer worries about these things even more but it's the director that has to deliver to the producer. If you are in a major movie and your name is something like Julia Roberts then you can ask the director whatever you like about how he sees the part, the story, the moves, the weather and he will take time off from organising the next set up, he'll be pleased to do it!

Most directors, if asked, `Can I ask you something about this part?' Will say, `Of course.!'

But the answer had better not be lurking in a part of the script you haven't bothered reading yet. Or indeed, can't be answered by the reply, 'It says here, you are very upset.'

`Yes, but... is she?.... could she be?.... shouldn't it be?..... do you think she feels....?'

`It says in the script,' calmly replies the director, `The script that was written by a person whom we have all chosen to trust to write the script...... that she is very upset!!!!'

No one knows why you are asking this question.

The Loader/clapper doesn't ask the camera person if he would rather not have film in the camera. The sound recordist rarely asks the director if he would like to hear what the actors are saying. They hardly ever discuss if the picture would be better in focus or not. They believe that the actor is performing another craft. It is and it isn't.

If the actor doesn't know how upset the person he/she is playing then who does? There could be lots of answers to that but the other question might be, who has time to explain it? The writer, who, for years has been told he writes terrible lines for women, wouldn't presume that he knows how upset she is! Anyway he's not there! Having written hours of TV I can assure you that the only shoot days I have ever been invited to are the ones where I have written myself an acting part. Other wise I've not been there to be asked, how upset is she? The director would know the answer but he's too worried about if it is going to rain again, and if it does, what will we do later today and all of tomorrow?

No, sorry love, in most cases you are the expert. You are the one in the right frock, you should know how upset he/she is. I've gone on too long about this but don't think like a theatre actor. There, three weeks is the least you will normally have to get your `acting' together. Why would you need three weeks on TV when no acting is required or desired.

Let's look more carefully at that.

Most of the guys that I know from The Bill are the same off screen as they are on screen. What a coincidence! The camera is an inanimate object, it believes what is sees. If you show it a police uniform it will believe that it is looking at a police uniform. If you show it a human being then that's what it believes it is looking at!

So what's acting?

Lets' divide the truths from the lies. The part calls for a Pathologist in his sixties.

Here are my truths....

Am I in my 60s?.......... Yes. (at the moment)

Am I a man?......... Yes. (though aware of his feminine side!)

Can I wear a suit?   Yes. (though I was once a hippie)

Am I vaguely middle class? Working class though been to RADA

Can I remember the script?   Yes, (easy)

Can I hit the marks?   Yes, (easy)

Can I sound authoritative?   Yes, (easy)

Can I arrive in plenty of time?   Yes, (easy)

What else is there? Can't think of anything so...

Here are my lies.....

Do I know about medicine?...No, (but the writer's medical adviser does)

Am I a pathologist? No, (but I know what tie they wear)

So where's the acting?

Let's look at an extreme example and see if it still works....

The part is of Hitler.

Male?   Yep.

Moustache?   No, but I can grow one in 2/3 weeks.

Can I wear a uniform?   Yep.

Do I look like Hitler?   No.... OK.... you don't get the part!!

It's that simple!

In the theatre I could be made enough like Hitler to get away with it... after all, a girl holding a comb under her nose and shoving her flattened hand in the air could look like Hitler.

Here's the real rub! In the theatre we might say, 'Yes, he could play Hitler but could he express the evil domination, the power hungry single-mindedness of the most notorious villain of the 20th Century?' Some might say, yes and some would say no. Depending on their faith in my ability to act.

On screen, those questions become irrelevant. On screen It would be entirely wrong to play Hitler as a villain! That's the job of the film. I doubt if he thought he was a villain. His villainy comes from mainly what he does.

In the movies what he does is enacted by another entirely different group of special effects artists or extras. We see people in camps, being carted off to certain destruction.... Hitler remains the nice friendly lover of Eva Brown... and his villainy is seen as even more horrendous. If he were acted as a villain he would be reduced to a comic book caricature, not feared or loathed but laughed at. Though, of course, there might come a time when he behaves like a looney... but even so, that is more dictated by the words, he will be given to say, rather than the excessive eye rolling! (NB: the management strongly disapproved of all of Hitler's actions, (he was a bastard) we are speaking of theoretical acting)

The terror of Silence of The Lambs comes from this chillingly cool person safely behind bars with unspoken powers and totally amoral beliefs. Anthony Hopkins acting is focussed on what he thinks the killer thinks.... not on demonstrating what the audience should be thinking about the killer. That's their job.

You are allowed to ask (quietly and when the moment is right) How big is this shot?

Television is very good at demonstrations. Cookery, Gardening, Makeover programmes our evenings are filled with demonstrations. But strangely those same cameras hate us demonstrating what we feel and think in drama.

Acting does exist, but it is a tiny part of a great jigsaw. The actor can only provide the bits of the jigsaw marked, `Pathologist.' (or `cannibal killer')

Just put yourself at the controls of a Jumbo Jet. A range of mountains looms several miles away. The pilot has been sucked out of a hole in the cockpit. The auto-pilot needs to be re-configured before the plane hits the mountains. You have a plane full of singing nuns and alcoholic screen stars. The person on the other end of the radio, who is trying to talk you down, is your estranged husband. The wind noise is enormous and the music is going out of control. Your job is to look out of the front of the aircraft and see the range of mountains..... being aware that soon you and your guitar strumming terminal patient and her co-travellers will be splattered across the side of a rock face.

All you can do is all you can do..... be aware of what has happened and look out of the windscreen.... the audience will do the rest!

In the theatre, you don't have any of the above ingredients, they will have to be imagined, but in the movie... they all there for everyone to see....

If the actor tries to act anymore than just a person fearfully looking out of a window, the whole thing will go pear shaped.

If you try to `act' all the above knowledge.... you'll look like the creature from the black lagoon... let us do the job and put the pieces together. It wasn't the best movie according to the critics (I thought it was really good) but it was one of the first disaster movies and the acting was great. Which really means appropriate.

I think Bruce is great at dirty vest acting but would he improve an episode of The Bill? Or throw it out of sync?

The trouble with actors is that we believe in a middle class work ethic. Work hard and it will be better..... But this rule doesn't apply to acting. Work too hard and the camera will wonder what you are doing. If you are working hard to be Hitler then that's what the camera will see.... someone working hard to pretend to be Hitler. That was the one thing Hitler didn't need to do.

It can't be that simple!

It might be!

Lets' go back to the theatre for a moment. Having started on time, 750 people have to hear the words, have to understand the story, get the author's message, get a drink at the interval, enjoy it, etc...etc... I guess this list could be endless.

And whose job is it to fulfil all those needs?

Well, there's the FOH team, stage management, the orchestra, the set and the actors. There once was a writer, director, lighting designer, producer.... etc...etc... this list could be endless too... but basically, however good those pre production people were.... the evening sinks or swims by our friends on stage.

The whole evening requires amazing energy, commitment, focus, volume, movement, and a thousand other things... and having done it.... you do it, with luck, every evening for the following three years.

CUT TO: Roger,

'Just look at the girl and lift your eyebrow, Roger,'

TURNOVER and ACTION! Excellent!! Really good.

I'm only joking. Roger is a great actor and I've always liked him and his work. And being Bond is not that simple.... but it is a different area.

On stage 80% of the actor's energy is going on his ability to make the audience look at him when it's his turn! This is not conceit, this is simply making sure that the audience is looking the right way and hearing the right things. I guess it's what's called 'presence.' You can't be a good actor on stage if you don't have the ability to make the audience watch you when it is appropriate to do so. Now let's go back and ask the camera if it needs presence. Well, it does, at least it knows what it likes looking at and what it doesn't but it will never see what it is not pointed at!

You can act your socks off if you like but the audience will never see it unless the director chooses to put your shots into the show.

So most actors coming to television have 80% energy left hanging in the breeze. It is not required, so it seems somehow magically translated into frowning! It should be focussed on thinking, not thinking acting but thinking thinking!

Let's think about that.

The script runs....'Have you stopped beating your wife?'

Short pause, thinks, says, `No, I haven't. ever beaten my wife!'

The answer required some thought...

but you can think without showing that you are thinking

or you can act thinking....

One great American actor when asked to be thoughtful or sad, tries to work out the seven times table in his head.

He doesn't ACT trying to work out the tables, he actually does try to work them out! Spot the difference?

What does the camera see? It sees someone thinking. The camera is not so smart that it can tell what the actor is thinking...but the audience knows what the character should be thinking and assumes that it's all happening. The camera and the audience together are clever enough to make sense of what is happening. If you try to add acting to that, the camera will wonder if there is anything that it doesn't know. It will invent stuff!

These are difficult subtleties. OK, let's see if it works with the words... most inexperienced actors think that it's their job to explain the drama to the audience. It's not, that's the job of the Radio Times. No explanation is required. Here are two things to think about....

Firstly all good drama is about conflict, the words in general being irrelevant. Clint decimates any script he receives. `Decimates' as Lord Bernard Miles used to say means cut down by a tenth or in Clint's case cuts down to a tenth. If the script gives Clint 20 lines he will put a pencil through 18 of them. I'm told.

Movies used to be silent, they still could be. Now I'm old, I struggle to hear what is being said in most movies. It doesn't matter... it's not about words! (don't bother telling me that Woody's movies are different, I know)

If what I'm saying is true, then the words that are left should really be important... `Make my day punk,' `Do you feel Lucky?' Say either line to someone who has just landed from another planet and tell them that Clint holds a rather large gun in his hand.... and they will understand! I promise.

Let's go further... in the theatre the actor might ask, `which word should I emphasise?'

Do YOU feel Lucky?
Do you FEEL Lucky?
DO you feel lucky?
Do you feel LUCKY?'

Will THEY sue ME for quoting those words from the MOVIE? Who knows?

Sounds silly to even ask about which word to stress. Just say the brilliant line... just say it! You can't say it without us understanding what it means. Unless you try to explain the 20 other meanings the line could have. It doesn't!

I love you, I hate you, I'm sorry. I'm angry.

There are a million ways to say each line.... but only one right way....

It's not to do with explanations, understanding, telling the audience how you feel, telling them what just happened, what's about to happen... it's one person talking to another, in one unique moment in time. If there are a million ways of saying the line then we have not grasped the uniqueness of that moment between these unique people. The writer chose this moment in time and space to get these words to be said.... I admit you could discuss what he might have meant.... but basically.... the `real' people in that unique moment are not trying to have an effect on an audience, they are trying to live from moment to moment... and it is that struggle which will have the effect on the audience.

Here's a good rule... to break if you want to... the moment the actor asks, What should I do......? Then too much is about to happen.

The camera sees very clearly things that are done! (great for cookery programmes) The camera prefers to see things that are!

I'll qualify that to make a point....

Big car chase... music, exciting, pace, speed, danger, white knuckle moments, gasps, breath holding..... now take yourself back to the day they shot it! Actually, one day's shoot would only have got you one sudden appearance of one car over the brow of a hill... showers of sparks, a swerve and a dust bin collision! That's all! It wasn't exciting to watch some guy doing this same manoeuvre over and over again, each time worrying about being safe! It was predictable, repeatable, totally safe and more or less, unless you were standing in the wrong place... boring!

That's the way movies are made otherwise they kill too many people. And whilst there are plenty of people to get through... particularly actors.... It costs money.

In most respects it's cheaper to keep it safe. I'm sorry if my casual joke has upset anybody... I can't help thinking about Roy and I don't mean to take this lightly. He was a sad loss. Sorry, Roy.

But now, let's add another part of the equation... perhaps this car is being driven, in the story, by someone whose eyes are misty with tears and whose desperation is tangible. Would it be better acted if we allowed a person in this state to drive that car? No, it would be better if the car were being driven by someone who couldn't act their way out of a paper bag but could drive absolutely accurately at speed. Hit the ramp, hit the marks, hit the spark button, hit the dustbins and then safely stop further up the street.... as someone shouts CUT! And then get ready to do it again, all day.

All of this can be applied to acting! We need dangerous acting, really dangerous, really dangerous and frightening..... by someone who gets there on time at 5 o/clock in the morning knowing the words. Do you spot the discrepancy?

Incidentally, how good and dangerous can an actor's work be if they are not there to do it? We think of the TV and Movie process as open-ended.... lets' do it over and over until we get it right.... true... but only as far as the schedule will allow. If the schedule says let's get that two hander scene in the can on Thursday... 99% of the time the scene will be done on Thursday.... and by Friday it will have been forgotten by everyone. Those involved in Post Production might still have it in their minds as they head for the moment when the actor forgets which tie they were wearing for which set up... but basically it's history. No more chance to do it better.

I'll forgive you for saying that there are some truly great actors who were truly dangerous. erm... Jimmy Dean! Dangerous acting, true. Died in a motor-car accident. We will never know if he could have been anything better than a very pretty dangerous actor. Sorry, James.

Serious acting.

The camera never lies. Yeah, right. What? Are you saying I really look that old and fat... , please. The camera does lie... but about certain things it is unforgivingly truthful. So I need to talk about real acting. The sort that gets people moved to tears and doesn't get laughs.

All actors have been in the position of having done what was a perfect performance, moving, clear, gripping, vibrant telling... etc... and they come off to be greeted by a people hanging around in the wings who shrug and say, Never mind there's always tomorrow.

What? I was great! I've never done it better!... I'll show those bastards.... tomorrow, I'll just mark it, I'll give it nothing... The following night they pick carefully through the text, doing absolutely nothing...

In the wings, crowds of well wishers, with eyes full of tears shower them with Champagne and rose petals and say it was the best thing since someone's Lear.

But I was just marking it!!

The point is, it isn't your job to cry... sometimes you may allow yourself the indulgence... but it's the audience who are there to enjoy the play. If YOU cry, they don't need to. The drama's job is to trigger off the responses inside a lonely sad audience. It is they who are to sink into the pit, and cry.

We have done experiments at RADA with crying and laughing.... the short answer, I expect you thought you'd never hear me say that, is.... that it is very very difficult to over act laughing...a bad actor might be able to do it, but a real actor would find it very difficult to over step the bounds of good taste with laughing... because we all long to respond to it, even if we are sad. That's why we corpse so easily in a tragedy... who cares if we do it in a Ray Cooney Farce.... Ray might not be best pleased but the rest of us don't care.

However, even very good actors only need to put thrupence too much acting into 'sad' and it is a travesty. (A Very Good Theatre in Edinburgh)

I will return to sad acting later.

Some more very serious notes on some very, very serious acting.
(Author's Message)

You might have got the feeling that this book is all about cheating. You will know for yourself, where you are, on the ladder of success. You might be a fully employed, fully trained working actor. And you might simply have got this book as a gift from your slightly dotty 'Aunty Dot' who thought you'd like a book on acting... instead of a slightly too small hand-knitted cardigan, made from the ends of many different coloured balls of wool... from the 'Grab a Bag' bargain bin of un-saleable wool in the High Street. By now, you might be longing to try on an ill-fitting cornucopia, rather than struggling with my restless prose.

Sorry, but, I'm now going to address the issue, of proper acting for proper TV. Not about cheating your way into the odd commercial.

Each of these notes could be argued over for a month, whilst sipping a fine red wine. Though both activities would give me a headache instantly. They are here for you to take on board your lifeboat. Or you could let them drift down into the cold Atlantic Seas, out of sight, tightly gripping the famous blue diamond. You must decide there is NO TRUTH OUT THERE.

Golden rule... if in doubt, leave it out. Even very good actors feel they need to 'get it right' and to address this issue they feel they need to do something... but are not sure what to do... do nothing, be somebody. Underplay but don't underbe.

This may not seem true but if you were to go back through your life, you would find, I hope, that most of the things you have done, were what you were meant to do!
In fact, this proves itself... because you did it! (there is no Parallel Universe. Obviously, I can't be sure about that. I shall be very cross if there is. Especially, if he ended up being the clever, good looking one!)

There is no Parallel Universe, so if you are finally playing the part that they gave to you. It is entirely appropriate that you should assume that you are the perfect person to play it. More than that, it is your duty to assume you are perfect for it! Embrace this thought. You are perfect, you are right, you are the chosen one... therefore, what do you need to do, to prove this? Nothing! It is a self fulfilling requirement. Therefore why do you need to 'act?'

You might feel you need to 'act' to be someone else. Why? If they'd wanted someone else, they would have hired someone else! Be true to you.

Think about this... Even if you did 'NO ACTING'.. would you become invisible? No.

You would still occupy a space in this Universe. And it would be you.... and at the very least ... saying the things that your character has be given to say. Relax the part is yours.

Steve Mcqueen, a great actor, never in his entire life, sat in a modern FORD motor car. And yet.. we have seen him back one into a garage. Of course, it's all digital... his job was to drive the car... did he ask the Director...

Is this a car yet to be invented and will I be sitting in it years after my own death?

Unlikely, and yet he does it really well. We like to think of acting as a mystery. It is, if you can't do it. But if you can, then put on the overalls, get into the cab of a lorry and everyone will believe that you can drive the thing.

A heat hazed figure on a camel rides over the horizon. Marvellous acting. Who knows who actually did it? Omar? Could have been, Probably wasn't.

Is this part me?

Yep, if your name is on the credits, then it is!

Who else could it be?

The guy playing the sheriff of Nottingham?

No, he's busy... playing the sheriff of Nottingham.

Commit to it.

We have recently all watched, Strictly Come Dancing. It's Great. Celebrities pretending to be dancers. Some of them do really well. But... we can tell which ones are bluffing... How? It is easy to focus on the dancing... but these notes are also directed at acting. Here is a list (with all due respect to the celebrities) of the things that we miss...

They find that they have their weight over the wrong foot.
Their arms and hands are not energised all the way up to the tips of their fingers.
They don't move from the centre.
Their faces are busy doing thinking acting.
They are never quite ready to change direction.

That'll do! Thank goodness they didn't go into the Big Brother House.

And let's simply tick those things off against a professional dancer.

The lines and moves they do are a linea stream of events from the first step to the last. So they are always in balance. They still 'own' their finger tips, even though they are a long way from their own space. They create a very big space, that they inhabit, around themselves, of which, they are the centre.

They know the routines so well that their faces don't need to show fear... just teeth. I know it seems crude to say it but as we say... tits and teeth! It means being there! Un-afraid. Almost daring the audience to take them on.. and yet not confrontationally... lovingly... (more of love later)

They move from A to B without expecting to be tripped up. They wouldn't spot a dog on the stage, until it bit their leg. They have committed to the moment.

If some of this makes no sense to you. Tough! Get over it. Just read on.

Allow 10% of your 'acting being' to hitting the mark. The other 90% perhaps should be redirected to the primary thoughts of the person you are being.

Not onto the secondary thoughts of the actor who is hoping to look like the part they are playing. This is tricky stuff.

Let's touch on crying again. This is easier for Women, than men.
No disrespect to either animal. Men defend themselves.... actors should never defend themselves. Perhaps that is why most male actors are more in touch with their feminine sides. Acting is about opening one's self to scrutiny and not being afraid. Most real actors are content with that.

So, big crying scene... the first thing I need to worry about are my eyebrows going off the acting scale.

Solve that! Cameras hate frowning.

American screen actors never frown.

Even if their wives are killed by gangsters who have planted drugs in their Police station lockers. They don't frown. So whilst you are learning the lines... stick some tape on your head, get it used to leaving you to do the acting. But we should be talking about deeper things than Sellotape.

Big Crying scene... whose job is it to cry? Well, it might be yours. It might be the audience. Let's look at both.

I have been in tragic real life situations, where there is nothing left but to cry.

There are times when the crying is so essential that you don't care who knows it...

I'm crying.

If things are that bad, you have to let go of your legs, and end up in a heap on the floor. In these cases, the frowning ceases to be a problem. Let it go.

But in less life threatening situations... the person who is crying.. doesn't want everyone to know they are crying. An actor must find inside them selves that one trigger to catch their breath... that one event in their lives when they can see the real most feared scenario.. and it just starts to stop their breathing.... we are at the point when a tear will run down the cheek....

NOW.... stop it.... don't let the world see you crying, that's what most people will do.... and yet... that will help the tears to well up... and it will go!

I have an image of the worst thing in my life.. I can create it in my mind's eye at a moment's notice. I feel guilty for exploiting this real event in my cheap attempts to create a fake tear. But as long as I know that I do it in respect and in remembrance of the one thing that was once a precious part of my now broken heart.... then the Gods of Theatre and TV don't mind. There is a price to pay for everything. Don't be sad... life goes on.. and there is no profit or logic in destroying yourself for something which cannot come back. No jokes for the moment. Just hold inside yourself the lack of breath, the bottom lip, the tight jaw and then the smile.. which makes us sadder.

Pull yourself together... it's only TV.

Mainly it is the audience's job to cry. You can't make them do that, you can only live through the play.... which might.

Years ago, during the silent move era, there was a little band, on the set, playing sad music... just to get the actors 'in the mood.'
Why don't we do that anymore?
Why not?
Because it made their acting CRAP!
It made them busy pretending to be sad.
They forgot that the audience were paying to be sad.

I don't know if it is true, but I believe that the iconic moment when 'Sam' plays it again for her, and she thinks through all those days in Paris, with Rick, in love, and a single tear trickles down her perfect cheek.... the director simply said,

Do the ten times table whilst we just shoot how beautiful and sad you look. Rather than anything more complicated.

They added the rest of the movie, they added the lighting, they added the very long held shot, they added the soft focus and then they added the music.. perfect. But it would have been too much if SHE had added all that. Just like Steve Mcqueen, who was just driving the car, she was just thinking.... not doing thinking acting.

Incidentally, you still have to hit the mark or you'll have to do it again.

If you were playing Rachmaninov's 5th, with all the emotion you could muster, would it matter if you hit a few bum notes because your eyes were filled with tears?

Yes, it would.

The two things that acting is, according to Paul Burge, and I don't quote accurately, anyone can do that.. I quote with great feeling, are focus and image. I've mentioned it but let me talk it through slightly more completely....

Focus simply means...

Who am I talking to? It seems a simple question. But to a Brechtian like me... quite a lot of it means talking loud enough for the rest of the audience in a theatre to be able to hear. It doesn't deny the theatrical convention, it accepts it and therefore doesn't lie. The Stanislavskians try to believe that the baby is real. On television, the baby probably is real. And so the focus can return to being... I am talking to Hamlet. The sound recordist is simply over hearing. Focus seems an easy rule to accept but as with most things I say... I mean them more than I say! Think it through.

Image is simply....

What picture is being seen in the head of the person you are playing? Poisoned Father? Dead baby? John with a brain tumour that makes him a genius.

Al sat down with a friend to have dinner, he said he could give her advice about her forthcoming divorce, he was about to order, then he realised he wasn't a real attorney, he was simply playing one in his current movie. That's image.

Old Lord Bernard Miles used to say,
The audience don't pay their money to see the play explained.
 They pay to see the actors cry, sweat and bleed.

Read the play book with the notes, if you need to have the play explained. Though I would recommend that you never ever do that.

The difference between Theatre and TV or Movies?

In the theatre you must take the audience by the hand and lead them on a magic journey to enchanted places. And in a way you must sell them a story as well as you can. You must pull them onto the stage and glimpse into their hearts.

On the screen you must try to hide most of those same things and make them come to you, for them to peer into your hearts.

Or you could say... just act quieter, smaller, neater, more intensely and don't move your eyebrows! And if they say you're too loud... they probably mean you are over acting.

Where do you look?

This is a vital question on Screen. The eyes have it. So they must be directed with great accuracy. In life you can look where you like.

On the stage it is obvious where to look. At the fireplace, and the other actors or at the Cherry Orchard, which we have decided this week, at Darlington, will be just above the Exit Sign on the left in the Grand Circle.

On screen the eyes are much more difficult. I can't do middle distance acting, if I do, I look like a photo of a person in 1923 pretending to be posh. So I must decide where to look. Not at the camera, of course, never, ever even glance that way, never! It will spot you. Some strange place in the sky? No, it will look like you are thinking acting.

For me there are ONLY TWO places to look. Into the other actor's eyes, and at the other actor's chin. And if I'm being really brave I can look between those two places. The distance between those eye lines is enormous.

Listen to the other actor and whilst listening, look at them. When you are talking to the other actor look at them. If for some storyline reason the pressure of their gaze is too much for you... then look away... but only as far as their chin. It sounds like I'm being unnecessarily dogmatic, only you can find out for yourself how little you could/should be doing. Obviously, if the killer walks in then you can turn and look at him... but always think twice about looking anywhere other than, other actor's eyes, chin or a specific prop.

The opposite to that very strict rule... is never let the camera see you being unsure where to look!

For example, always try to count how many steps there are for your grand entry. If you have to look down three steps up from the bottom... no-one will believe you when you say, Ready for my close up Mr De Mille.

The camera also doesn't like you looking for your mark. Always ask for a mark, if you need one, but never be caught looking for it. If you are entering a mid shot and the focus is critical then get them to place a chair for you to stop at. So you don't need to look, you'll feel it on your legs.

If you are walking from a distance... and you're not saying anything, then count the paces back from the mark. If you count back ten paces.... then walk forward only nine, since your forward steps are longer than your backwards ones.

The camera likes to see either full faces or profiles. If it is possible, always try to cheat as full a face as you can towards the camera., without moving your mark. If both the camera and the person you are speaking to are in front of you, then just slightly favour the camera but keep solid eye contact with the other actor.

If the camera can see your eyes, and you don't know what to do with them, imagine how much the camera enjoys watching you wondering what to do with your hands!

It never bothers us in real life, but the moment you stand in front of a camera, you become a hand wringing, gesturing, windmill. Leave them alone. Try to pretend what a real person would do in your situation... impossible... go to the library to see what people did before Television...

(That was a joke... don't do that!)

You are a real person...

Actors are real people...

Have you ever eaten with one? (Mel Brooks)

A lot of acting is the way you say the words.

This sounds stupidly simply but... we can't tell if you can't act as long as you are walking around like a human being. The moment you open your mouth to speak.. then we know you can or can't do it. But what makes that difference? It's not the quality of the voice. It's just the way you say words.....

Dave Courtney, the celebrity gangster film producer, says that the best acting is done by adulterous husbands. Guys that couldn't act their way out of the proverbial... seem to be able to tell the biggest whoppers, without a glimmer. The best liars... and some would say that acting is lying... get to the point where they actually believe their lies... this has to be true of actors.

One famous director will often rehearse his actors, for some time, without letting them do any ACTING. He will stop his actors the moment they DO the slightest thing with their voices or faces, or intonation, or dynamics, etc..

He insists that the words are said as dully as possible... as a monotone... as a dirge.. as a really bad actor might be tempted to do it. The frustration is enormous... the temptation to DO ACTING is over whealming. And by the time he lets you DO ACTING... you have realised that the less you do the more the camera hears and understands. The viewer CAN be trusted to understand, your nuances, even if you try to hide them. And particularly if you say the words... accurately.

The word HATE, is still hate if you shout it, whisper it, stress it, spit it, scream it, sing it.... or just think it!

Take your time.... the director will cut it down.

TV doesn't tend to go in for very long monologues... in a way every tiny line is a monologue. The author put each one in for some purpose, so it is important. Not important enough to hang the whole drama onto, or for you to oversell, but important.

Golden rule: you are always saying this line for the first time!

You have learnt it, rehearsed it, practised it.... but now when you need to say it.... don't ever forget that it is for the first time. It should be kept like a violin string.. tight, taught... the camera hates slack acting. That taughtness also goes through the silences... perhaps even more so.

Everything is a journey... the line, a paragraph, a monologue. a duologue... try never starting that journey where you know it will finish. To be crude... if you are going to end up 'sad' try embarking on the journey happy... we pay to see the actors take the journey. Discover where you took the wrong fork in the road as you are travelling and as we watch. It works perfectly in soaps, too much. The moment that Sonia and Pauline are really enjoying each other's company you know that someone's about to die.

Never go to the toilet before a take.... it will give your over-active imagination something to worry about instead of embellishing your performance.

If you are going for the big scene and you feel, as I always do....
I'm going to do too much here...
Don't blow it, don't blow it.
Dig your finger nails into your hand, don't draw blood, but feel the pain and then.....
SHOW THE CAMERA NOTHING... and do the words.

This way you can trick the camera, even a very expensive one, that something is going on inside, too deep and mysterious, for mere mortal cameras to understand.

Obviously, if you are a truly great actor.. then ignore all my advice and get Aunty to knit something else for Christmas.

Lets learn some lines.

I once did a play directed by a great theatre director, where he rehearsed the play for three weeks... not letting the actors say any of the lines, insisting that they continuously improvised the world, in which these 'Camus' people lived. He was quite an old hippy in his youth. He then rehearsed the play as written for just the last few days! I didn't mind. I only had one line, the last line of the play, and I couldn't help learning it. It was 'No!' But the importance of this story, especially for TV acting is that you will never really rehearse it... so you really need to be able to learn your lines in a void. You won't be able to relate it to your move to the sideboard to find the gun.

You may not be able to scribble it on the front of the news paper you read in Act Two. You won't be able to associate it with the arrival of afternoon tea.

Incidentally, Golden rule: In the theatre, always suggest to the director that your character likes tea and cakes in Act Two. Its worth a try and it helps the touring allowance to go further.

What was I saying?

I have a terrible memory. If you don't, then skip this bit, you won't understand it.

I have a terrible memory... but I have done 'walking cover' duties on some really long plays, playing both main parts. And It didn't give me a moment's worry. I was always ready to go on.. though I never really wanted to. I was too busy using my West End Dressing Room as an office. Here goes.... stick with me...

Firstly let's remember a list of say 10 objects. And as I write them actually visualise the object I'm placing next to the number

One:	The object is a large number one...	1st prize
two:	Two fingers up, like Churchill.	V
three:	A set of cricket stumps	III
four	Four dots on a dice	::
Five	A shark eating the five on channel 5	
six:	Someone being sicks....(sic) (it's getting strange now, I know)	
Seven:	Someone in seventh heaven, an angel.	
Eight:	A gate with a giant 8 wrought ironed into the design.	
Nine:	A clock face and the time is nine.	
Ten:	The door of Number 10 with the PM.	

That will do for the moment, since remembering lists of objects on a table is not the same as learning a script. This is just a starting point.

Now I can easily ask you which was the sixth object.. and you will instantly see, I hope, someone being sicks.
Or what was the tenth object... obviously the number 10 door.

Easy, if you couldn't remember them then you are clearly... not paying attention. That was the easy bit! Those objects and numbers are now the foundation to remembering any list of objects.... because if I now give you another list of objects you can easily place them next to the first easily remembered list.

Here's the second list... as you read them place them next to the first list of clearly seen objects....

I have picked these out of my 'Learn to speak French in ten minutes' book. Which I have owned for twenty years... and so far mon French is Mauvey. Why do they have great long sections in the book about 'This is my uncle he lives in Paris?' When the chances are, that if my uncle actually did live in Paris, he'd have taught me French from an early age!

I'm only going to Paris for le Weekend, no-one is going to want to know about my uncle who is dead and lived in Norfolk! Calm down... that's for another book.

Here is the list....

Horse, ball, picture, chair, car, stairs, book, actor, dark, cup.

I put 'actor' in, just as a bit of fun. Though, I'm, in fact, quite cross at the moment. Mainly because French people use the word person for nobody. And the Germans use Marmalade for Jam. I'll get over it in time.

So that's the list of things, easily learnt but let's just be sure we can learn them accurately. by placing each one in a compromising position next to our first list. Stick with me...

A horse with a 1st Prize rosette, sorry that was too easy... just luck...
Ball being kicked by Churchill.
A picture of a cricketer at the stumps.
A giant dice sitting on a chair.
A shark driving a car holding the five logo in his teeth.
People being sicks down some stairs.
An angel in Heaven reading a book this one perhaps, and she might have recommended it to a friend... who also liked it... sorry, got carried away.
An actor leaning over an old Eight gate. (Bernard Miles perhaps)
It is dark, street lights, etc. A clock strikes nine.
The PM comes out of number 10 holding a cup of tea.

So if you needed to recite that list of things it would be an easy job to conjure up your first list and simply see what is next to them....

Which is number 6? People being sicks down some stairs.
What is number 10... a Cup....
What is number three... a picture... of...

Of course, you may say to me...
Why don't you go to Spain for your holidays? Or you might say...
I could have remembered that list anyway.
And I would say, well, I told you clever dicks to skip this chapter!

You might have remembered them, in a linear way...

So, a Horse, who is the 1st prize, is being ridden by Churchill who is playing polo with a ball using stumps for the goals, it's a picture, behind which is a giant chair and dice, though the chair has a shark sitting in it because the chair is in a car and it's going down stairs with lots of sick people, one of whom is an angel reading a book, probably not this one, past an old eight gate with an actor, in the dark, his watch set at nine, drinking tea from a cup with the PM .

Either way it was an easy list of things to remember. Don't for the moment worry about the effort it takes to put all these things into your brain. It's like putting index cards into the computer... it takes time but once they are there, the information is easily retrieved. My system, if you decide to adopt it, is very labour intensive at first but it is hoping that once the information is typed in, it will be able to printed out without mistakes or hesitations.

So, two ways to remember things.... association with a 'standard' (you can write your own) aide memoir list (hey, I do speak French) and association of one thing next to another in a linear sequence... with or without the 1,2,3 etc. List.

But now comes the tricky part let's learn a piece of text...
no, let's not, it's too much bother.
I'll just give you an outline of how I approach the text.... That's just for me.
I know I will have to learn this speech three times for it to stick.
I know that, so I know there is no point trying to learn it all in one go.

In the game of Pool, you can earn extra visits to the table, if, for example the other player misses a ball. So if you have a shot in hand... there is no need to pot the ball with the next shot. You can simply use the next shot to line up the ball and the pocket...leaving you with an easy pot.

It's the same with learning the words... no need to do it in one go... just get the clues lined up first... then test the clues.

I must build a scaffold for the words.
I have to test it... if it fails...
I have to build a safer scaffold at the point where I fell off last time. And then, when I can recite the words ten times without referring to the book... I can then start to forget the scaffold. The building is finished. Now I can get on with the acting.

Don't get me wrong... learning the words is the lowest part of acting... but if you can't do it, then you CAN'T ACT.

This way I reduce the learning the words to a simple function, once I've finished with it... I get on with looking the other actors in the eye, not referring to the book, and moving around the stage like a young gazelle, whilst the other old boys are still saying. Sorry, everyone, I knew it yesterday.

You didn't, you silly old sausage... though on a good day you might be able to bluff your way through it!

An old actor friend of mine still goes home to his wife at the end of each acting day saying....
Phew, Got away with it again!
He means the acting really, not the words, but nearly the same thing.

So, if you are tired skip this bit and wait until you have a difficult script to learn... here are the headlines. my theory is... that if you can remember the first word... and there is an association between that word and the next, and then there is an association between that and the next... then theoretically, if the links are strong enough, you should be able to write the first word on a slip of paper... and that, by association, will take you on a journey to the last word of the play. And it does.

It takes planning and effort... but it is better than hoping the play will get learnt by osmosis.

The rehearsals are not for learning the lines they are for rehearsing the play.

Here is the simple first long sentence.

I have taken it, arbitrarily, from a book about acting. Let us assume that it is a teacher talking to acting students....

TEACHER: *(to class, She is still quite pissed off by the French student who thinks that chairs are feminine, what about Chippendales! She thinks, then she goes on smugly....)*

"Pantomime is a waste of space on TV. It doesn't matter if the actors are from the Old Vic or from Corrie. TV doesn't like what it doesn't recognise."

My copy of the text would, during the first stage, look like a road map, perhaps of Belgium. See illustration... 'Pantomime' is, I've decided to connect the 'i' to 'is a' by simply common sense, as the start of a sentence, and I would also draw a musical 'slur' across the words to connect the 'i' s. The 'a' in waste and the 'a' after 'i' is connected so the first three words are remembered.... I admit this is pedantic!! very pedantic... but it needn't take too long... the first four words are fixed in my brain. I will never, ever have to remember them (or forget them) and their relationship again. 'Pantomime is a waste....'

Don't say to me, this is stupidly easy... because if you do, I'll say. Well then learn the other 40,000 words in the acting book and see how long it takes for your osmosis to run out of memory. There is a long monologue (or whole play) ahead of us. We don't just need the first four words.

'of space on TV' I see that as 'o' something, 'space' has a letter in it that looks like an 'f' and then another 'o' something TV. You need to make an association between the shape of the four words their letters their meanings and their context. I also see the 'c' in 'space'

Pantomime is a waste of space on TV.
It doesn't matter if the actors are from the
Old Vic or from Corrie.
TV doesn't like what it doesn't recognise.
Even the documentaries, about men who
wear dresses, feel and look very
un-comfortable.
TV visits to the Circus leave us wondering
why so many people still tour Europe
in caravans and tents.
Surely, it should have been made illegal
years ago.

as an incomplete 'o' so there are three non perfect 'o's in the four word phrase. That is the first sentence. Good, full stop. Now let me test the scaffold....

Pantomime is (that was easy I wrote the first word down) The next feature is waste (because of the 'a' preceded by an 'a' so it must be Pantomime is a waste.... (of what... of..space) of space (where) on TV. Pantomime is a waste of space on TV. I won't go any further because I can sense your eyes are misting over and wishing you had taken the course on 'Inland Revenue forms of the Forties'

Mnemonics! That's the word. That's what I do, a word at a time, a paragraph at a time, a scene at a time... a collection of mnemonics, similar sounds, similar letters, common sense, visual scribbles to connect two different things, pictures in the margin that relate to the text... anything that makes concrete a verbal thought.

The next stage is to test...

Put the script out of reach and face down... this has to be a real test... not a squinting out of the corner of the eye test. And if you forget something. Go back to the scribbles and figure out why it (the scaffold) didn't work, simply make the connection better.... so if I keep forgetting as one often does the first word of the next sentence. normally because there might be a sight change of thought... look at the link more carefully...

Pantomime is a waste of space on TV. It doesn't matter if the actors...

If I can never remember the next line which is... 'It doesn't matter....' I would think about IT as being the ITV (which I have just said!) and then come back to find 'It...' once I have found the 'It' I would find the 'doesn't matter' either in the sense of the retrospective association with the collection of 'nt's and 'mt's in 'doesn't' and 'matter.'

Yes, my brain hurts too. This needs to be mastered if you are slow at learning lines, because although it looks complicated, the brain will DO THE WORK for you. If you give it the right tools. Don't give up. I promise you it will work if you take your intellect out of the process. The scribbled text page will give you a list of the things that I think work, but you must do it for yourself. It looks a mess... but it is to do with getting it into the brain logically.

Incidentally, the theatre director I mentioned, now 40 years older, always makes his actors learn the lines before he even starts rehearsals and has done that for most of his career! The play to which I referred, earlier, he tells me, was just a ploy to get the actors to think outside the box. If you need to learn the lines before the rehearsals, as you always do on TV, then you have even more reason to get the learning done and not confuse the line learning with the job of acting. You can't begin to do the second before you have mastered the first. His other tip, when reading lines from the book early on in theatre rehearsals, is to hold the book upside down! It makes the brain think laterally, literally.

Please let's move on and talk about something else.

Remember : Focus and Image.

That's really all you need to know. But it might take a lifetime to 'get.' Who am I talking to? What am I thinking? Speak up! Don't bump into the furniture, remember the lines and don't tour in the winter. Have I said any of that before? I have a terrible memory. As she says in 'Chicago' I'm older than I ever intended to be.

Chapter 3.

Comedy.

We have just finished a second series of a show called Shoot the Writers! For ITV1. It was a comedy sketch show for brand new writers. With a company of brand new actors. Why wasn't I asked to be in it? I hear you ask. Tough.

Sorry, it's a tough world, I meant to say, and I think you were busy when we were casting.

But just in case we meet at the next casting and assuming that ITV1 don't decide they would rather have someone famous, here is my take on acting comedy.

Don't do it!

Do the job but don't do the acting.

Comedy is a funny thing, not very often in television but it is a very difficult thing to get a handle on. In our show we basically separate it into three areas. The first area is funny actors. There are actors who have great difficulty not being funny. So in many ways writing for them is a piece of cake. They pick up the script and they make it work and they make it funny by what can only be called the force of their comic personalities. The second kind of comedy, the kind we need for our show, is writing where the situation is funny. The words are not funny in themselves, sentences taken out of context would not appear funny but they are only funny when you know there is a dead cat in the next room.

And the third kind of comedy which we tend to get too much of, particularly in the UK, is based upon the pun! Or scenes which end with the instruction to pull back to reveal notice saying.... dyslexic something!

I'll try and talk about how to deal with each.

If you are a funny actor, then the chances are that by the time you are 20ish you will have recognised this. It normally comes when the headmaster of your Drama College pleads that you, 'Please, don't play Shylock for laughs.'

Don't assume though that this will be easy for you to play comedy. It doesn't mean you are a stand-up comic and that people will fall over when they hear you talk. They might not, even if you are a stand-up comic.

Comedy, even superficial comedy requires there to be a basis of recognition that it is taking place in a real world.

My favourite Comedy anecdote, to help us learn the nature of comedy, comes from the 19th Century. A famous couple of old British actors used to tour the States, with their comedies of manners. At a certain point in the play the husband asks the wife for a cup of tea. We don't need to know WHY this line is so funny. We can assume that some sequence laid down early on in the play makes the asking for tea to be hysterical! For forty years on tour, audiences all over America would fall about at the request for tea. (you could stretch out the same tired old material for a life time in those days) Eventually, the line got progressively less laughs, and less and less.

The husband kept accusing the wife of distracting the audience, by tapping her foot, or doing a gesture just as the joke was being set up. 'No,' she claimed she was doing nothing to distract and the laugh failed, through his fault alone
.
'I'll watch you tonight, like a hawk,' he said. That evening the play went as planned.... she notedly froze at the appropriate moment and he asked for a cup of tea.... nothing!
'Why am I not getting the laugh?' he roared, after the show!

'Because,' she said, 'You USED to ask me for a cup of tea... NOW you are asking me... for a laugh!'

Few things are less funny than a comic asking for the audience to laugh.

Blackadder doesn't think he's funny. Basil has no concept of humour. Fletcher does have humour, but his need to get the laugh is a private matter, not to be shared with his inmates, he uses it, to keep himself sane. Del Boy is good natured, but he's not trying to be funny, he is trying to survive.

Pantomime is a waste of space on TV. It doesn't matter if the actors are from the Old Vic or from Corrie. TV doesn't like what it doesn't recognise.

Even the documentaries, about men who wear dresses, feel and look very un-comfortable. TV visits to the Circus leave us wondering why so many people still tour Europe in caravans and tents. Surely, it should have been made illegal years ago.

Horses for courses.

Live pantomime in a theatre, might not be to everyone's taste but just relax and watch the faces of those around you.. it's a wonderful explosion of communal energy, the colour, the dancers, the men dressed as women the girls dressed as boys, the interactive shouting, who knows what it all means? Even old cynics can appreciate that this touches us in a very deep place in our pagan hearts. A community shouting for justice, shouting for a common goal of love conquering adversity, shouting that he's behind you! Show this chaos to a camera, however, and it just doesn't understand.

The circus too is breath taking... if you can really see how high that very pretty semi-naked girl is, swinging above the heads of the audience. And we can gasp at her nervous steps truly risking life and limb. We can see the distance she will fall, and they sometimes do.. All these things on TV are wasted. The girl is inside a box on a stand in the corner of your front room, who knows how high she is off the ground, she isn't really that naked, she is wearing a rather tatty pink body stocking, it's cold in tents on the Russian plains, and is she really pretty? Not that that is the point I hasten to add, but simply by watching TV we are not really there and can't share certain experiences.

So we need to think quite carefully about trying to work out some rules for trying to get this conundrum right.

One of my comedy heroes was Mr Pastry, Richard Hearne, I knew he was what I wanted to be. And for a while I was but it was never going to last... no one puts Mr Pastry in the top 100 iconic comedians. The camera can't understand him. It sees the wall paper table, the paste, the bucket, the ladder and.... the camera thinks, 'Please, don't be stupid, don't do that!'

The top 100 comedy moments mainly contain things that the camera didn't predict. The fall through the bar, (oldest gag in the book) but the camera was surprised.

'Don't mention the war!... I nearly got away with it!' It's people, in places, at the right time.

Man with Dead Parrot... the camera didn't see it coming. Four Candles, the camera couldn't be expected to understand... but at the root of it... people do lean on things that are not there, their parrots do die and they could say Fork Handles.

But it has vary rarely been recorded in history that a man putting wall paper on a wall has walked up the paper dragging on the ladder. In a theatre we have bought into another kind of suspension of disbelief. The audience would laugh, though they seldom do, when Caesar dies, but they would if they had bought a ticket to a different theatreland invention. They buy into a conspiracy... they join the conspiracy...Other wise they'd all shout out, 'Brutus is behind you!'

It is true, on the other hand, that one notable audience did shout out, 'She's in the attic!' during a performance of Anne Franke, performed by an unappreciated 'celebrity actress.' They knew what they were doing.

There are very few comedy heroes who have gone down in history because of their ability to make funny faces... give me a moment while I try to think of one.... yes, there are a few, Rowan Atkinson, Jim Carey, Gene Wilder and probably a few others but... you'll know that they are really good actors behind those gymnastics.

I've done long runs in the theatre in funny roles and the one thing you quickly learn is that as you hone your craft and try other ways of getting the laugh bigger, better, differently there comes a point when all the audience sees is someone trying to be funny... they don't like that. It's like watching Wayne Sleep trying to jump higher. He is a great dancer, he might like to jump higher but the audience don't pay their money to watch him trying!

I'll say it again:.. don't try to be funny.

If you are a funny person... relax, you are a funny person.

If you are not a funny person then you stand a much greater chance of being funny if the situation is funny and you are not aware of it!

It goes back to good acting, the villain is not required to be aware of what harm he is doing to others. The central role of a comedy is normally the one who doesn't know what's going on, who's in the bedroom, where is the vicar, surely it's not the day that the in-laws are visiting? All these things are nothing to do with the actor.

The funniest things I've seen in the theatre were nearly always the most serious. Corriolanus is hysterical if the helmets don't fit. But it requires a comic genius like Tommy Cooper or Freddie Star to simply get the laughs from the wrong helmet without Shakespere's seriously funny play.

But there is timing, let's see if we can decide what timing is. It's really that fine line between taking the audience with you... or letting them get ahead of you... or letting them fall behind. Bradley Walsh could read the telephone directory to a live audience and by timing the end of the lines get the laugh, people respond, just like a dog to Pavlov, to the rhythm of a statement. Rowan's list of school boys! Maybe they can still hear that old joke that uncle Jack used to tell many Christmases ago. Hear the tone of his voice, feel the steady set up, the hesitation, then the button neatly placed where no-one under the age of three was expecting it. In the same way we could smell the turkey on the range and knew we were about to eat for the year.

One of the terrible things about TV comedy is the need to leave a gap for the laughing, without hearing the laugh, that the audience will give it. The second least funny thing is leaving a pause for a laugh that doesn't come. On Television there will always be laughing, even if we have to put it in ourselves. Experienced comics would never leave a pause... they would carry on with something that resembled a pause but in fact was a real noise or action that could carry on and fill the gap left by the silence. Nature abhors a vacuum, comedy abhors a silence, though I don't mean only in an audio sense... the thoughts carry on.

At an audition don't try timing, you've either got it or you haven't . but give it time. Nothing puts a director off more than someone who is so slick that they have already worked out the business!

If only comedy shows were as funny as out take shows. But they are not. Because what the camera needs is TV reality not faked hilarity.

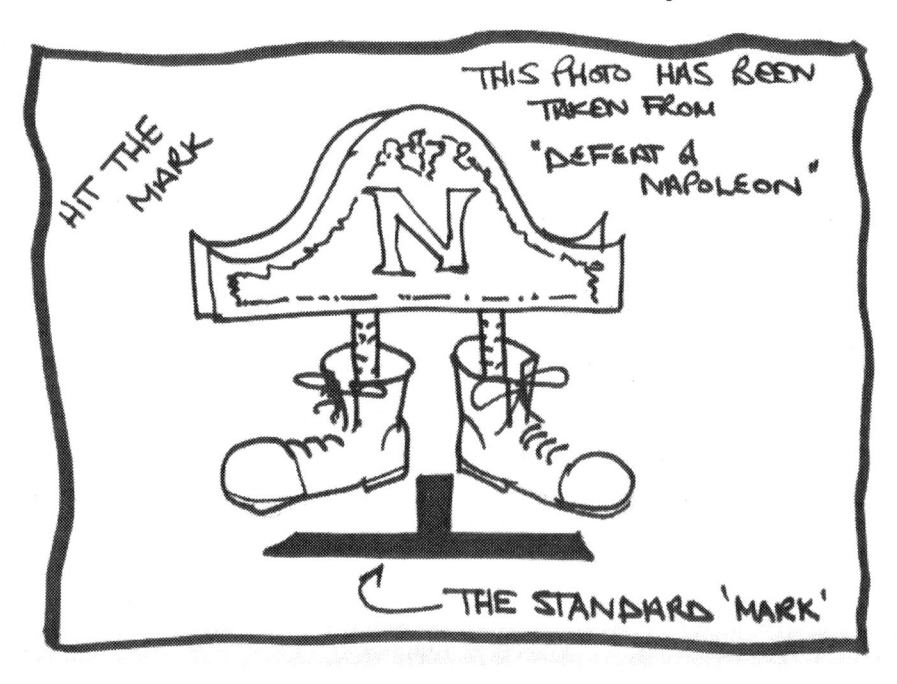

HIT THE MARK

THIS PHOTO HAS BEEN TAKEN FROM "DEFEAT A NAPOLEON"

THE STANDARD 'MARK'

So for those of us who only think we are funny and maybe we are not... be cautious.. if you have the slightest doubts... then simply play the moment... force yourself to 'act better.' In other words... when the line requires a double take kind of pause before the button... don't count 'one, two' under your breath... think through the pause, what the character should have been thinking through his/her pause. 'What did she say?' 'She... is the pilot?'

Whenever the writer has indicated, or the director asks you to put a beat in prior to the end of the line, for effect. Never put a beat in! But think a concrete thought that lasts a beat.

I know I've said this before but it's worth reminding myself that it is not the job of the actor to explain the plot... or make the audience laugh (it is, but not as a pro-active function) it is the job of the actor simply to be that person in that situation and behave accordingly... which might explain the plot and get the laugh, but only incidentally.

I can hear roars of disapproval coming from the back of the room where the cheap comics are sitting, throwing inkblots at each other. Shut up, and sit down, or you'll be sent to Mr Hart!

OK, one more time... great comics can make up their own rules about how, why and when to get their laughs... but the rest of us need to have a safety net... it explains to us when to pull back and get the laugh instead of mugging till your face drops off. Go back to the 'truth.' Obviously not the real truth... the real truth is you'd rather be at home with a cup of Hot Chocolate. But the fake truth that you don't know the widow is in the cupboard wearing your prospective Father-in-law's pyjamas and where you are about to hide your fiancee from the Vicar. Ahh truth!

I often run a short course at RADA (I mention it enough) for theatre actors who wish to learn more about TV acting... I don't just do it for the money, honestly... I want to give something back... as they say... I hope you can spot the sincerity in my voice. But sometimes we get the occasional actor through our doors who simply CAN'T ACT. (one of the greatest crimes known to mankind, you'll agree)

Let's think for a moment about how to help them get through this difficult maze of rules to see if we can help them..... to be able to ACT GOOD.

Pause for a long moment. (not counting, not thinking acting, just thinking)

No, sorry, push off, we actors are busy. We can barely find enough work for us.

But... here are a few thoughts. Stand still! Don't shuffle! Read whole sentences, never single words! Can't you hear how dull your voice sounds! Move it up and down!

To BE or NOT to BE, that IS the QuesTION.

No, No, please stop, you can't act. Please leave the class. Go and see Sally on your way out and she might let you have your money back. But I doubt it.

I'm glad they've gone!

Let me talk for a moment about the writing of comedy.. because it does help to identify what is important for the actor.

Chapter 17.

Let's call this Chapter 17. It's not funny or clever but it is pointless to think that any of the things we are discussing can be separated from each other.

Writing comedy has to start with an idea... but don't assume that it has to be a funny idea. It needs to be an idea about which you want to write. The nature of the Universe, congestion charges, income tax, the Mayor. Brain-storm a complete list and then leave it alone to go back to, once you have exhausted all you have to say about the one you picked. Move quickly, don't beat yourself up about not being able to find anything to write about Ken, just pick the next one on the list.

I am sure that the most time lost in writing is lost choosing what to write. That sounds fair enough but. .why not simply say the next hour is to chose what to write... then the following hour is to write it. I'm not explaining this very well, am I?

I'll keep writing until I work out what I need to say. And then I can easily cut it... the most important part of that, I believe, is simply to do it! Don't find reasons not to do it! That's easy... let's stop for tea, OK.

I feel better for that, though the writing hasn't got any further but I do know now where I'm going!

Just let me remind myself why I'm writing this. Acting is a tough task master. Because you are either in work... with the consequent benefits of having new colleagues/friends you have something to learn, you have something to perform and you have a credible existence in the world.

Or, you are not, and there is nothing more sad than an actor having to say that he is not currently working or is waiting for the phone to ring or there are many, many things up his/her pipeline.

I personally would rather you didn't work in a call centre, unless you really enjoy it but even then I wouldn't want you to tell people you do it. But the conversation looks better if it goes.

What are you?

I'm an actor.

What are you doing at the moment?

I'm writing a few comedy sketches for Shoot the Writers! The late night Cult Comedy Sketch show produced by Colin Bennett.

I thought that was over.

Yes, but that was just the second series.

Are they getting another one?

Erm... They are waiting to hear, should be soon.

Didn't it get dumped because it looked cheap and.... .....

Look just mind your own business. I've got to get back to my Call Centre, it's a busy time of year... Gas doing electric and phones doing drains and stuff....

they're waiting for me...

Sorry, that conversation didn't turn out quite like I'd expected, I was rather hoping it would have been more positive.

Here are the list of notes we sent out to our prospective writers... these were just our requirements, not to be confused with someone else's. But there is a global truth to them, if you are a previously un-published writer.

Lots of what I have put in the writer's pack below is worth thinking about as an actor.

A Few Notes on Writing for TV

Writing for Television is easy.

Getting someone to read it is impossible!

Tricking a TV company to pay you for it is almost unknown. (sounds just like trying to be an actor, but worse) We use more actors than writers.

I exaggerate slightly, though only you will know by how much. I know many people who earn a living writing for TV, (I used to be one myself) but none of them started yesterday.

It took years of getting it closer and closer to what THEY (you know who they are, don't you?) wanted.

Any scripts sent to us for use in Shoot the Writers! (at the time when we are looking for new scripts) are read with great interest. But any scripts sent to us for projects that we are not making, are of no interest whatsoever.

Be focussed. Who do you want to write for? What do you want to write? We are sent too many scripts for 'Little Britain.' That would be great, if we were making Little Britain. We should be so lucky. We have no idea what we'd do with the money. Make one series, sell the rubber suits on Ebay, and then retire!

Our needs are very specific. If you don't write stuff that fits what we want then... hard luck, but we are saying that very pleasantly.

Briefly what we need is...short, easily shot, easily located, funny, non personality, 'written sketches' with punch-lines. We like surreal but they can't simply be 'hippie stream of consciousness' (save that for your book about acting) it still has to go somewhere. We have to like each sketch on its own merits.... our cast of actors tend to be in their early twenties.(though we are not averse to putting a grey wig on them)

And that's it!

TV is a very sound-bite medium. A good sound-bite has a beginning a middle and an end and lasts no time at all.

We only have time to know new characters if the slot is longer. Like in a Sit Com. No-one is going to get you to write a Sit Com! Unless you have written several successful Sit Coms. TV executives are not brave, they are trying to hold down a really tough job. None of them will get sacked if they get John Sullivan to write their next comedy series starring Frank Skinner.

If it is terrible, (and it MIGHT be) people will assume that John and Frank were just having a bad write day and move on. But if YOU wrote it (assuming you are not a leading TV writer) and it was terrible, your commissioning TV executive might not work again!

So you can see why it's so difficult. That's why you have to change the way you think about writing.

There is a wonderful play called 'I remember Mamma' written by John Van Druton. The Mother in the play takes her daughter, an aspiring writer, to meet a famous author to seek advice about becoming a real writer.

The famous lady asks.... 'Does she want to be a writer? .....Or does she write?'

I think that's great! No-one should aspire to being a writer. (it might be wonderful to be famous or lauded or admired for one's writing talent.)

Having that or not having that shouldn't have anything to do with the actual process of needing to WRITE. You are already a writer! If you write. (You ARE an actor who writes, if you write)

So you write, but who cares?

I write! My grammar is terrible, my syntax is nowhere, my split infinitives have indifferently gone and my spilling is appalling. But I write and people pay me for it.

Why?

Because I write what THEY (you know who they are) want! (not what I want)

I admire the people who write what they (themselves) want. I am jealous if they get paid for writing what they (themselves) want. But they have learnt to play the game.

So focus.

If you love Mat Lucas, write for him, send it up. If you love George Lucas, do the same.

Never get them the wrong way round and never send it with a letter starting Dear Sir or Madam, and never spill their name wrongly. Obviously, I can, because my spell check has gone wrong, and if they sue me I can say... 'Oh, no, I didn't mean Matt Lucas... I meant Mike Lucan.' And if in doubt, finish with a look to camera, (laugh) move on.

Never send generic writing off to anyone. Send them what they want to read. Does this takes research!? Yes, No, not much! Look through the TV guides for whose doing what. Look for people you want to write for and write for them.

And by the way there are no rules and anyway I know nothing!!

It is important that the characters in your work are instantly clear through the writing You don't need to spend too many words describing them. It will be cast.. to someone else's wishes...

Be practical... You may set your sketch on the moon with camels... but... producers will be more drawn towards easy wit rather than complicated props and locations. This is true of all producers requirements.

Set your sketches in very ordinary places that can be found cheaply. Some can be more surreal if you like.

But, Shoot the Writers! was the cheapest programme on TV, let alone one that uses writers and actors....

If you think you are a surreal specialist... you'll serve yourself better by including a couple of 'bankers.' Producers are not always able to spot genius when it's wrapped up too tightly.

Be practical... a small cast, will give better lines to fewer people and be easier to shoot. Avoid anything that requires in-depth pre-production preparation.

Your artistic integrity is important ... but the Producer's decision will never be made irrespective of cost.

'Falling over a Banana skin' is sometimes funny... but as a writer YOU need to be responsible for the humour rather than leave it up to a funny actor. Steer clear of complicated stage directions.

We know we are old fashioned but we like a 'pay-off!'... or punch-line... but it's not the law! Just think about when the audience should give the big laugh, which we tend to like at the end. But don't let that stop you from starting with one and then doing other laughs on the way to the end!!

Max Miller's rule was start with your best joke and end with your second best joke. We try to do that in Television... what used to be episode three might be transmitted as episode One, if we think it's funnier.

Don't waste too much time with 'padding' we would prefer a short script that we need to pad with action rather than a long script that we need to edit.

You must be prepared for Synchronicity as we are...meaning that however unique your writing is, someone else will be having the same idea at the same time. it's just life!! Get over it!! And write something else.

Don't 'quote' from other works... by anyone other than very old, very dead people... I'd like to thank everyone I've quoted in this book, please don't sue me... I'm hardly making any money. What little I'm getting is for a retirement that I have only just started to think about.

One last thought:

No-one, and I mean no-one, buys writing or acting from someone they don't know. So get to know more people and get to know what they want (even if all they want is to be left alone to retire. Goodness, that sounds inviting.)

The end of the writing stuff.

Sorry about that writing stuff but I want you to go out and write plays! And then ask me to be in them! (not produce them) This is the important point.

No-one wants you to be a successful actor. Only your father, and to be honest, he'd rather you joined up, and became a soldier serving in war ravaged Iraq. And your Mother wants you to tidy up your bedroom! How does she know if you are staying in for something to eat? You're not going out wearing torn jeans, are you? This isn't a hotel! Or maybe they want you to learn a skill, like.... there aren't any OK!

I've yet to meet an expert Plumber! Let alone someone who knows how to run a Hospital or School. So get over it! And write plays that you can star in!

Here is my list of rules about starring in plays. So that casting directors can come and see you and send you up for TV dramas... It's a great idea! But you may not be able to get every casting director to come.... There must be a way.

Casting directors are advised to look away now!

Let's look at your fringe play. Never do a play that you can star in, if it only features you! If you were a busy casting Director, What would you prefer to do...? Sit and watch Holby City and see ten new actors or spend a cold/hot evening in a dump watching just one!

Write it for a cast of at least ten friends. If you can't write a play then someone in your ten might be able to, that's not the important point... let's all agree that Cameron Mackintosh will not transfer you to the Piccadilly. Agreed? Please, I promise you he won't. So it's just a vehicle.. which you can design.

What are it's design features? The actors, the title, the handbill. That's all we have to sell, not the set, not the costumes, not the music, these are only of interest to the people that see the show. The first/only thing is to get them there.

Pick a title that will appeal to the casting directors... I don't know, but what it might be.... erm...'The Casting Director's Handbook'
'Casting for the Big Fish'

I think I could write both those plays, (2 days maximum) don't worry I'm not going to.

Tell them about how many good actors they will see if they come.

Make it easy for them... somewhere easy to get to. Never ask them to pay for a ticket. If you are in the West End and you can't get comps, it's worth getting the ticket for them. They will offer to pay if they can, but it is much more important to you that they come to see it, than it is for them.

Never, never work in a tatty fringe venue that has dirty toilets, Casting Directors hate that! Clean them yourselves if need be, make it a selling point... we've cleaned the toilets! Don't assume that the land lord cares.

Go through the book and target the ones who will be able to get there easily, geography. They don't all put PO Box addresses.

Target the ones you really like. I mean the ones whose work you have seen. And write saying that you liked it... and say that your play is similar.

Try and build up a head of steam, a letter, then a hand bill, then a phone call. Don't make it look like you are stalking them, they hate that! But all these three mentions of the play, place and time could be fortuitously synchronous.

Make sure all members of the company pull their weight.

Local papers might be interested.. write the story for them! Being an actor is not interesting, there is no story there, but there might be a local connection. After all you are writing the play... so make one. Why write about Catherine the Great if she never visited the Jumping Jack Pub Theatre in Catford. Someone else, like Jack, might have done.

If you don't want to write a play then pick a play that is out of copyright. Cut the boring bits and insert new bits designed around your actors. Pick a long lost play by a famous person. Casting Directors will have seen all the plays ever written, don't make them sit through another Romeo and Juliet. They won't want to. They won't come.

Don't forget you might also be doing this to get an agent. You could write a play called.. 'The Agent's Handbook' or 'Agent to the Big Fish'

I could write both those plays, (2 days maximum) don't worry I'm not going to.

Let's talk about agents for a moment.

Getting an agent is impossible. My agent of the first twenty years of my acting career died suddenly. This was the lady who would always lie about me. It was great, she had a way of making me think that going to the audition was a matter of form, just for them to take a look at me, to confirm their already made choice that I was their man. So I always went to the audition in a calm and confident mood. It was never the case, of course, they had never heard of me, and didn't know me from Adam Ant. But it did help my attitude to the process. It made me un-afraid... and I got a few.

As a very famous Casting Director, says... what we need are, 'Actors who are un-afraid.' This form of words is truly on the money.

One of the great mysteries about acting is that overweening confidence and EGO are not what is required, even though the media might give you the impression that they are. The media don't cast plays, thank goodness. Though I'm not doubting their ability at raising your profile to the point where you might get a foot hold in theatre or TV but be aware that it could just be to get into Big Brother. Which you might like, and good luck to you! But....

Actors who are un-afraid.. simply can do the job, are confident, not too confident, humble, but not too humble, brave, not too brave.. and can act!

So my agent dies. May she rest in peace. She had used the client's money to make some improvements on her home... it would have been paid back... if she hadn't died. I didn't mind. So for that moment, I'm without an agent.

I'd been, by then, in the business, working regularly for twenty years or so... semi-famous, or at least I'd been the leading man in the first West End production of Chicago. Had written a West End play and starred in various TV shows. But could I get an agent? Could I heck as like. A friend of mine who has just finished having a nice part in a Roman Polanski film has also just looked for an agent, could he find one? Could he heck as like!

So we know it's tough. You know it, and I know it, and my friend knows it, and his neighbour knows it. (his neighbour is a famous TV director, but will he repair the adjoining fence, will he heck as like) But it does happen. The most important thing is that you have to aim, at where you are in the business. You will never get a lead in the West End until you have been in the back row of a West End Show. You will never get a lead in a movie unless you have played the quiet gangster. (there are exceptions to these 'nevers' but they normally only happen to Big Brother Contestants, and first division footballers, get over it)

So you will also never get a top agent unless you are a top actor. I got, in the end, a very good agent, by recommendation, and we are very happy together (my first agent always used to say that it was a marriage) I think she is a top agent. But we both recognise that Max Clifford isn't trying to get me to open super markets.

So try the co-operative agents first, if you are just starting out. You must be in Spotlight so take Spotlight's advice, they sometimes know who have places on their books. And of course, write to them all, just for a meeting. If the letter lands on the right day, it will click into place. Carma or is it Karmer or is it Calmer? Or is it... oh, I'll look it up in my Astrology Book.... it's Karma! I don't know what it means but something like...

Laugh and the World Laughs with you. That's the showbiz comedy version, it's more like.. be good and good will happen. And it's TRUE. You will get an agent if God, or whoever runs this wacky little planet, wants you to.

You have to Do all you can. All you can is enough.

I will spend a moment talking about how to decide if you should go with a certain agent or not, but don't be cross if you don't have any choices. Go with the one who wants you.

Never go with one who wants money. That is not how it works in the real world. Never go with one who wants to get your photos done for you, by them, at your cost. Never go with one who wants to sleep with you. It doesn't work. Never go with one who can't remember who you are. Think seriously before going with one who has never seen your work. Never go with one who has more than 30 clients PER MEMBER, of agent staff. Think seriously before gong with one who promises you ANYTHING! Never go with one who wants to meet you in a seedy hotel.

Children are often cast from photobook agencies, so I am not assuming there is anything wrong or dubious about that, that is children. Parents have another long list of cautions to do with their children. I'm assuming they will have the good sense to work those things out for themselves. Just like life there are nice people out there and there are monsters out there. Luckily in the real business called show, there aren't many real monsters. But maybe I'm naive.

In the end... you are looking, and so are they, for a long term relationship of trust and mutual admiration. So if it feels dodgy, it probably is.

The other important point is that Agents never got anybody any work. Really? They put you up for things.. but you get the work.

At best, they might have suggested you for a part in a company, as a package, with a famous actor who is already on their books. This does happen. But other than that, not having an agent doesn't stop you being employed and having an agent doesn't stop you being unemployed.

Be a member of Equity. You should be a member of the union, like you should have a good agent if possible. But neither will get you work automatically.

But you must be in Spotlight!... or you are not an actor.

Agree a protocol with your new agent. How often should you ring them Sometimes, once a week, never. Agree it and then do it. But don't bug them, they know you want to work, they do too! They will need recent photos, that look like you. They probably will do mail outs if you are in something worth shouting about... offer to share the postage.

I am very happy with my agent. Most actors are, though they also like to complain about stuff, and will always consider that my agent (or your agent) is better than theirs. The grass is always greener, till you get there, and you then discover a man on the credits called a Greensman... whose job it is to paint the location's garden GREEN!

Let's talk about Showreels.

This is a tough one! The Americans love them. And if you have done some significant work in the movies, and some television, there is no reason why you shouldn't get someone to dump a few clips across onto VHS/DVD ready for the moment when they are required. But they have to be good quality. They have to be short and easily watched. They have to contain sensible work, (not that appearance you made as Sydney the Serf in the back of a shot that nearly included that very famous girl.) And you must never send them out to anybody! Unless asked for.

Imagine this, a busy office, paper and photos everywhere... and a pile of unwatched videos. When are they going to watch them? The phone never stops ringing... OK take them home... do you know how much fun there is in watching a dozen tatty videos? I do, there isn't any. And now think about what to do with them once you have watched them. Send them back? At a cost of 3 first class stamps and some packaging. You might have sent a puffy envelope with postage on it. Who knows where they've got to, they don't make an office any easier to make tidy! They keep falling over.

AND some Casting Directors really get cross, at having to deal with it. The ecological implications alone... of all that tape, being dumped, being re-used... being re-posted... and feeling guilty! Never make someone feel guilty. They hate it!

If someone asks for one, then pay to have one put together. But it will need to be updated as soon as you get another job.... get a Video Software package and do a rough assembly onto DVD. But don't burst a blood vessel making it the best and most exciting quickly cut movie presentation of your appearances in The Woolpack, playing someone you have called Freddie the Farmer.

It is a serious investment, make it if you can afford it, get it ready to be made when someone asks for it. But for the moment, it is not a daily way for actors to get Agents or Casting Directors or Directors. It might be soon. The Actor's WebSite is a growing trend. Actors do tend to Email a link to their site...

I don't mind hitting the link and arriving at a CV and Photo. But is it really that easy? The CV is there but the photo needs to be downloaded it takes three hours because it is SO GOOD. I hate being logged on so I never get that far. Americans do like web sites and DVD showreels.

More and more business is done on the Web, but most agents and Casting Directors in the UK prefer to flick through a hard copy of Spotlight. I apologise for those who love the new media. But we still deliver broadcast tapes to ITV1 in old fashioned cassettes for them to transmit the show, with VHSs for them to watch... and I think it will be a few years before they say 'download it to our server.' Digital doesn't really exist. Please don't get me started on that!.

Finally, Here is something that will really need your ability to learn words in a void.

Corporate Events.

Corporate Events.

What are they? And why don't I get more? Actors not only work in the obvious places. They also work in entirely unexpected places. For example...

Acting out corporate messages... or role play on behalf of corporate clients.

Exhibition stands, where demonstrations need to be done.

Hosting evening events for clients.

Wearing Chicken outfits.

There are thousands more but that is basically the corporate world. I used to dislike the very thought of having to do one of these jobs, before I knew how well paid they are. So there was a time in my career (huh) when I used to tour around Europe being the European expert in 'Asynchronous Transfer Mode in Corporate Networks.'

What did I know about it? Nothing... only the words! Which is everything!

There are so many different types of corporate work, that I won't bore you with the finer points of them all.. but here are the highlights.

Why do they need actors?

Because they can't do acting, and they need people who are confident in public areas. It is astonishing to me how frightened corporate people are, of the world in which they live. As the CEO lands on the grass outside the Hotel they all seem to lose their ability to string two words together...

Luckily the actors (who don't give a damn, and know that however important he is in the world of IT infrastructure or grommets, he can't ruin their career) are not phased by his/her arrival. This is worth money.

It's really great to be able to wear a smart suit and let other people really think you mean it. You stay at a much better class of hotel. And they feed you regularly.

There are two things I have learnt about doing corporate lecturing. For a start it is easy. An expert has basically written down what you need to say and now all you have to do is make it exciting. He couldn't do this, even though he salivates at the very thought of Internet Protocols.

The real bonus, is to be able to get the chance, in a very hostile environment, to learn how to control a crowd. How to take them and guide them through seemingly impossible technical notes and MAKE THEM LOVE YOU! It's an incredible feeling. And it really focuses your ability to be someone else... believing something that you patently don't believe and can't understand. How is this trick done?

Here are the rules...

You can't make someone love you! You really can't.
But they can't stop you loving them.
In a safe environment, like a corporate one,
where there is no chance of acquiring a stalker, People feel easy enough about letting the person 'on stage' or 'on camera' seduce them. This is not to be tried by anyone working for the corporation. The safer you make them feel, the easier it is for the seduction to stick.
You can't make them love you.
But they can't stop you... loving them.
And so.... they love you... and contrary to the rule...
You made them do it!

The power of having the camera or the platform is so easily lost by someone who doesn't know how to work the game.

The actor must always be in a receptive mode to seduction... it is part of the craft... of getting work... of keeping work.. It is that simple mind set of being open and not hiding anything. It means of course... in a very general way... love everybody...

That's why we are called lovies!

Sorry, I've gone all warm inside... I'll just go and dig my finger nails into my palms.... Ouch! That's better.

There are no clear ways of getting corporate work... but in general most of the people who put on these shows and events don't know too many actors so... you must find them and I think the first and best way... is to be 'local'

Find the local Events Organisers, and introduce yourself... they might already have a few actors that they use regularly but ... if you are just around the corner... one day it will click into place....

Contrary to what might be the advice to actors in TV, like never sending CVs to Directors or Producers unless asked.

In the corporate world it is acceptable.

Give them a reason for seeing you... like your 'interest' in their product. In the corporate world your main friend is the Corporate Producer who will then get used to using you. And of, course, there are specialist Agents.

I once recommended an agent to a student of mine, he had a particular area of 'expertise lecturing' (I could have done it!) and he now earns 100,000 a year... imagine, if you can, how pleased I am for him.

For a moment let us remind ourselves of what we mainly need to know as actors on TV....

There is a lot. And yet...There is nothing. Just keep your voice down and stop your face from joining the circus. I could go on for another 46,000 words but I'll save it for my next books.... make up... real acting... the theatre... winning the lottery the easy way... and philosophy for the stupid.

I hope this book has informed and entertained you. I know there is loads of stuff I should have said... and loads of stuff I've said too much about. You really do have to decide what to do about your foolish obsession with getting to act on screen. I hope you make it. And if you don't I hope you find something really good to do with your valuable life. Stick with it... and just do it. It's a great world. Constantly changing...

There was a time when the world was flat.

It looked flat, it seemed flat and all the intelligent, erudite, thinking, chattering classes could prove it was flat. Current scientific belief is that it is not flat but round. Things change. The 'facts' of one century prove to be the 'old wives tales' of another. There is only one thing that matters and that is what you think. First do no harm... then the rest is open for you to decide for yourself. Have a great life on the screen, in the theatre, on paper.... but mainly have a great life... in life!

My thoughts go with you!

Time for me to go to bed... bye bye everyone bye bye.

Here is some more... could be a glossary.... please read it though to the end.

Glossary

TV TERMS and few theatre terms thrown in just if I feel like it..... and where they have been referred to in the book

I was going to put them in alphabetical order but I don't want you to look them up, just read and move on... it's not important....

A Pea Bulb, Pag Light, Baby, Inky Dink, Key Light, Ground Rows, Floats, Back Light, Vari Light, Par Cans, Red Head, Flood, Basher, Blonde, Brute, Arc Lamp.... they are all lamps right?

From small to big and even then they'll invent a few more and of course numbers...243s. etc. Even Lighting Designers and Electricians can't keep up with the new lamps. So don't worry you don't need this. Recently, shooting an episode of a long running TV Drama, in a studio with millions of pounds worth of kit they pulled out a fluorescent tube screwed to a bit of plywood and stuck it up in the face of the actor. How do you reproduce terrible public lighting? Put some terrible lighting on it.

Arri, that's short for Arriflex the standard pro cine camera, not for major motion pictures but good enough for TV films. For major motion pictures, the kind I don't get.. they use.... really big ones.

Atmos, short for atmosphere, normally related to a sound track, though could also be used to describe the use of a smoke gun. It'll add texture to the final feel of the work.

Autocue or Portaprompt, Brand names for kit that brings the words up right in front of the lens, so the presenter looks efficient. How do they remember all that stuff? They don't, they never do. Most people talking straight to camera will be reading the words. Acting is never done this way... or shouldn't be, but occasionally for corporate work where the words are too boring and long, we might give the actor a break.

Baby legs, a short tripod camera support. and legs in general.

Barn doors, doors to stop light spilling from the lamp onto places where it is not required.

Billing, this is not just, 'Name above the Title' Have you noticed those one screen, black and white, lists of credits on trailers for movies, where everyone significant is mentioned. This is a contractual agreement to do with names and their relative sizes, implying their relative importance to the movie. Billing is also how the Broadcasters refer to the way the show is described in the TV Times.

Cuey, That's what it looks like if we have cut to the 'Talent' just slightly too early, before they talk. Acorn Antiques was great at this.

Mark it, That's what the Director or Assistant says to get the scene identified on film or tape, normally by putting the slate in front of the camera. Or the tape marks on the floor to show where you need to stand.

End Board, Putting the identification for the scene at the end rather than the beginning, for convenience or reasons of sensitivity.

Bubble, endearment for Light Bulb. Bottle, endearment for camera lens.

Contact sheet, call sheet, , For the actor the most important of these is the call sheet, it tells you where, when and what. If you don't know these things then you know nothing! The contact sheet is also very important to you, save it. It will give you everyone's name.... remember these names... The Director, the Producer and the Casting Director. Above all the Casting Director.

The Camera Card, Is the Camera Person's version of the script. No dialogue but shots, types, numbers and positions.

The Camera Script, is the last version of the script, this is the one everyone will work from on the day. It might well be in Shoot order rather than story order.

Backlot, The bits of the Studio that can be used as the fire escape, or road or warehouse. Almost every movie and some TV shows contain some Backlot shooting, We do it a lot on Shoot the Writers! it's worth trying to spot it. It's normally a location that only just looks like what it is meant to be! Just.

Cheat eye lines or positions, the camera hates it when the actor is looking in the wrong direction, even if it is the right direction so sometimes we cheat the eye line, by making the actor look at something irrelevant, but specifically chosen for it's place, so it looks right.

Bars, tone and Clock: This is all the stuff at the front of the TX or Broadcast master tape, that we occasionally get to see by mistake.. the bars and tone come first and represent perfect colours arranged in vertical columns so that we can all agree what we think red looks like! This is more important than it appears, because there are hundreds of different reds, and we must agree on one of them on the assumption that most of the other colours match up. And tone is a 1kh noise that is really annoying and seemingly too loud, set at -18 on the digi Beta scale so that we can all agree what is considered loud... a reference signal by which all the other volumes in the show are adjusted.

Domestic Cut-off, this is the invisible parts of the domestic picture that we don't get to see on our TVs. The full size picture the camera takes is slightly bigger than the one that gets shown at home, that is why we are so keen for actors or action not to be too edgy, otherwise no-one will see it. Be aware of where you are holding the murder weapon.. don't wait to be told, not in front of your face, not in front of Frost's face, not out of vision.... but until told otherwise... hold it close in to your own face without obscuring it. If they then want to change the position of the held knife then they will tell you. Try and line the object up with another object in your view so that you can mark the place for yourself... in mid air.

CSO, Chromakey, Keying, When I first started writing this book in 1896 there was very little CSO or Keying. In fact I wrote show called Captain Zep for the BBC which was the first example of 'Drama' using CSO... where the actors are superimposed on a graphic background. The world has moved on a little since then... from Jurassic Park to Narnia... but it all started with and still requires Keying to remove one background and insert another. The Americans tend to call it 'blue screen' but it can be any colour as long as it is clean and even.

Credits: This is the End roller or Crawl or list of people working on the show. For a half hour show it must never be longer than exactly 30 seconds roughly. The list tends to start with the 'talent' working down the level of importance, then back up the levels of importance. There are no unimportant credits. But there are very strict rules about who is allowed to go on. For example, one person is not allowed to have more than two credits... so it might say: Written and Directed by Colin Bennett, even if he also made the frocks, put the tent up, and carried all the kit. (which he almost certainly did)

Crab sideways, track forwards, tilt up or down, pan left or right. These of course are camera moves.. but you never crab forwards and you never pan up. Etc.. though sometimes one might say it wrongly, you don't get sued.

Fade, mix, cut, wipe. Ways of going from one scene to another. Fade can be up from black or to white, either way it is a gradual change of pixels, so the picture softens from one to the other, if it is between two actual shots then it is called a mix. A cut is simply a sudden change from one to the other in no time at all, a straight cut. Either very un-noticed between two people talking in the same space, between their reverses. Or very quick and numerous between scenes to add dynamism. A wipe is a fancy slide, of a thousand different types, from one picture to another. We don't see them much these days, though Lucas still likes them in the on-going Star Wars Sagas. (George that is, not Matt)

Cue: These are simply the same as saying 'action' which we tend to use on film or location, but in a TV Multi camera studio we tend to say 'and Cue Sir Laurence'

Roll to record, Turn over: The most important thing to remember is that this really is time to get ready to act... the camera and/or recorders need to be fully up to speed before they can be recording properly. It is during these moments when you need to prepare to breath. I'll just take a moment more to say that this moment between hearing the words, 'Turn over... to Action' are those moments when the professional actor really girds his/her loins.

We can all throw a dart at a dart board... some better than others... but for the pro dart player... this is the moment when the whole audience of 1000 people stop drinking and shouting and all watch that tiny space of hog's hair called 'double something to finish.' That is when the real pro knows the time has arrived to pull one out of the bag. The same with acting... up to the point when 'Roll to Record' is called the crew are laughing and talking, the generator operator is whistling, the make-up person is blowing talc' into your cracks, you are relaxed and smiling.... If only you could do your scene now... it would be perfect.. but then it all goes quiet. You could hear a pin drop. Everyone turns to look at you. You have to hit double top. These precious moments are for you. They are secret moments for the actor to fill their lungs with air, fill their thoughts with image and focus. It is in that five seconds you learn about your part. And then it's gone and the Cresta Run has begun. Just learn to treasure that moment of calm.

Depth of field, focus: The part of the picture that is in focus. If we are shooting an eye, in a very big close up, then the highlight on the eye ball is the part that might need to be in focus, but the eye lash might be out of focus. It looks better than the whole thing being in focus. So the depth of field is the distance between being in and out of focus. It is important to stay on the mark in these situations, obviously. Don't sway, STAY.

Director/ Producer: The Producer is the man in charge, he hires the director, and between them they hire everything else. There are many different types of producer, Associate, line, Co- and various others. basically they are the management. Unlike the Director who is in charge on the floor. The Director dictates the shots and it is generally perceived to be his/her creative imprint on the show that makes it work or not. He will hardly ever tell you what to do. Because he will want to talk to Marlon. Having said that... don't forget NEVER to talk to him. Make sure you have plenty, though not too much, eye contact, be ready for eye contact. But pressure from you... he doesn't need.

Establishing shot, though MCU to BCU. It won't always work this way but just to get a feel for what the scene is about they will want to shoot the wide master, this, in the edit might be the shot they first come to and the last shot they go to. They may want to visit a few times when they decide to cut the scene down or remove a boom in shot. (The mike on a pole hovering over your head, it sometimes drops slightly into the top of the shot, which often no-one notices on the day. Were they all chatting up the make up girl whilst you were acting?) The rest of the are definitions of size of shot. Mid close up, Big close up, mid two shot, (two people) etc. The only one you need to worry about is the CU or the BCU, the closer the shot less movement you are allowed to do and the more important it is to hit the mark. Don't forget you are allowed to ask for a mark, not of the director but of a guy in a baseball cap. You are allowed to ask the camera person, in mime, how big is this shot? By one hand above your head and the other showing the bottom of the frame, across you chest. The ONLY other thing you are also allowed to ask is, Whose 'action' is it?, if it is unclear to you. In other words when someone shouts 'action!' do you start talking or do you wait for the empty horses to be brought on.

Cut away, pick up. I hate cutaways and pick ups but if you don't take them you regret it in the edit when you find you haven't got anywhere to cut to during the take when you almost got it right but stumbled, or if they need to cut the dialogue. It is a safety shot of something irrelevant like hand wringing, or door knob holding, foot tapping, that can be placed anywhere in the sequence. You can spot them a mile away but it is better than a jump cut. A pick up is simply where you need to get a certain bit of a scene but can't bear to attempt the whole sequence again from the top. So you might be told to pick it up at the line where you cocked up, for the last ten takes. You will surely get it now it is the first line of the sequence? I'm sorry, it might not have been your fault, it might have been a continuity thing.

Flag. You don't need to know this stuff. But it is a bit of black metal, cardboard, old copy of Heat magazine, something flat used to screen off some extraneous light, like a barn door but can be used anywhere, not only attached to a lamp.

Hair in the Gate. It is never a real hair, well I suppose it might have been in the 70s. But generally it is a stray bit of emulsion that has been caught up in the frame by the mechanism. It is truly wonderful to me that we still make movies... on film. We can never be sure who really invented it. That long strip of highly inflammable celluloid or whatever, covered in emulsion and light sensitive bromide stuff being roughly pulled through a slot by a couple of brass sprocket hooks in front of a glass lens that Newton would have recognised. He can be thrilled that in this Digital age we haven't quite yet replaced it! So the occasional mechanical blip is forgivable.

Time code: That is the reference by which all is measured.. it is like the footage counter on your old VHS, (still the workhorse of screenings in offices all over the world in TV) But time code obviously relates to the time rather than the footage. It is expressed in terms of Hours, Mins, secs and frames. Most camera masters start with a single digit to express which tape is being used, but most TX (transmission) tapes in the UK start at 10, preceded by bars, tone and clock and ident. American standards are different.

The strange thing is that when you buy some footage from the states say just 5 seconds of helicopter over NY. When you try to fit it into the 5 second gap you've left in your UK programme, it won't fit! Even though there appears to be no difference in the speed of the helicopter!! One of those eternal mysteries like weighing a sparrow in a plane.

Foley: Is the process of inserting dialogue in a movie. With all those explosions, car crashes, and sprockets clacking, mainly in the movies, the talking is re-recorded later in Dean Street. The system is called ADR. It is time consuming and tricky stuff to get the lip sync done accurately. The Americas are great at Dialogue Replacement! But then they don't tend to care what the actors are saying. We over-act, like RAF pilots!

Gaffer, Best Boy, This is the chief lighting man and his son. We have 'best boys' in most departments these days. Apprentices, of course. On a recent trip to South Africa I discovered that to ask for Gaffer tape was not considered PC. So I now call it Duct tape. Which is what they say in the States. For sealing up air conditioning Ducts! And a thousand and one uses on a TV or film set. Mainly to... stick things together.

Grips: These guys push and pull the camera. Only when required of course! It would be silly to employ someone to just make life difficult! Though come to think of it...

They tend lay tracks, set up tripods and everything to do with the easy movement of the camera. As I've said before. This is the most expensive part of filming or taping. 'Turning Over' is the easy part... the rest is waiting.

Lighting Cameraperson: You can guess what they do. But there is sometimes a distinction between the person who operates the camera and the person who lights the scene. Sometimes not. But they also have a small team of loader, clapper, focus puller. Sometimes they are the same person. But each job is distinct and separate. A big film camera needs to be loaded with film, quite often. It is a skilled and very, very important job. No point in loading new stock without checking the gate... and the inside of the camera needs to be kept pristine.

The clapper (boy, in the olden days, of course,) runs in to ident the shot and scene and take (saying it out load as well as showing the camera the slate, where all that stuff is also written). He then 'marks it' by gently clapping the board. The sound recordist has the noise of the clap and the Camera has the picture of it happening. Two machines can then record separately but their end result can be synced together in the edit.

Gobo: Not the nickname of the loud bloke who seems to know everything, though there is always one of those. But a pretty cut flat metal sheet with holes to simulate leaves, or church windows, through which to shine light, to give the effect of.. whatever. You can also make them of bakofoil if you're stuck. They are a very simple but very effective way of changing the feel of a place.

Headroom: The space in the frame above the actor's head. With ratios of 16:9 or 14:9 or 4:3 it is a significant talking point. Not for you but for others!

Ident: This is what the person with the clapper board says at the shoot. It is also the information on the clock which appears on the front of the TX tape, just after the tone and bars finish. It states the name of the show, the episode number/name. The production number the Aspect Ration Code number and all the timings... show starts at 10:00:00:00, Part one Duration 11' 23" Part two starts 13:00:00:00 Part Two duration: 12' 36" And the Production company details so that they can phone you that the tape has failed its tech check or QC. And it does! Sometimes.

Post Synching: The Dean Street excursion... extra days money!

Noddies, Reverses, Long shots, Close ups, You know these. Noddies are shots of someone nodding! These are for cutting into a scene where you need to cut or edit, which you can only do whilst watching someone else! Reverses are the two main shots of any scene... firstly we take the burglar talking, then we move the camera to take the policeman talking. When we cut it together it looks like they are having a real conversation... even though the burglar who is appearing in Les Mis this evening has been let off early to make the matinee, lucky devil!

Long shots are taken from a distance, someone could even stand in for the burglar in this shot which we might have saved, so that he could go early. And of course we cry in the close ups! Though not if you are just playing the pathologist.. that would throw the whole story off.

Rushes BITC on VHS: When the film or the tape comes out of the camera, it must be looked after at all costs. So the director must make his first paper edit or rough cut using something less expensive. So there is always a version of the camera masters made in VHS, with the Burnt In Time Code (Said like bitsy). His decisions can now be made frame accurately, rather than cut when the guy gets out of the lorry. He can now write that up. Either on the back of an envelope or electronically, so that the editor can make a start on an Off-line or Rough Cut. Which are both early stages. In fact getting to this early stage is really easy and quick.. so it is always surprising to those who don't do it how much more work needs to be done to turn it into an On-Line, which is the finished product ready to be transmitted or Printed.

Some of the stages to get from one to the other include, (though as they say, this list in not exhaustive) Tightening up the edits, making the skin tones look matched, putting on the music, sound effects, then doing the audio balance (this is the longest job of all, it all needs to peak just below 6 on a PPM) Then captions, legalising. Adding all the bars tones and clocks etc.. the paperwork which is extensive. EG: Does the show contain imaginative ways to commit suicide? List the Swearing and its Frequency. I often think about some innocent young youth employment scheme person going home to tell their mum that they spent the day making a list of the most obscene language they had ever heard. I don't think they give them that job! But someone has to do it!

Stings, Gongs, Bongs, buffers into and out of... Stings, of course, are short bursts of music to make you think something is happening. Gong, I'm told by an old actor Friend comes from Mr J. Arthur Rank's Strong man banging the gong at the opening of a British movie. Nowadays it means the early parts of this week's episode where it says... 'previously on Doctors....' just to remind you of what happened last week.

What's to know.. ? sick people.. .neurotic doctors. Bongs and Buffers (sometimes bumpers for sponsors to claim the show as their own) tend to be the opening sequence of a news programme and the EoP1 and Pt 2 captions and stings to announce the commercial break.

TX is simply short for Transmission, Though I can't remember why. Many of these things come from certain regions at certain times. Like we call a 'Darlow,' someone who is in a show but never watches it! We still like her but it did make us a bit cross at the time. Or a Sally Power: A small power pack for lights.

2,4,6: Just a block of wood, made like a little flight of stairs. .2" then 4" the 6 inches high. Just to raise something into view. Or a million other things.

Wildtrack: This is a recording normally of atmos or ambience. Taken 'wild' with nothing happening. Someone will shout, 'Quiet everyone!, wildtrack, side of the railway, take one!' and then everyone will remain very quiet whilst the sound man records seemingly nothing for two minutes. This is used to repair holes in the sound track where there might be actually nothing! You can never have real nothing on the sound track, even though you can't hear anything.. you must always have wildtrack nothing!

Up stage foot… the one furthest from the camera or audience. It used to be up the slope of a raked stage.

Rake: Sloped stage.

Mark it: Either a bit of tape in the shape of a T showing where the actor should stand or a very under energised performance just to get it done, quickly or for cues etc.

Dry: forgetting the words. In TV there is always someone checking what you say, you need to be…

DLP: dead letter perfect.

A Gnats: A very small distance. If they ask you to move left a little... they mean a very little... 'a gnats' a very small part of a very small creature.

FOH: Front of house people in the theatre, not back stage.

Walking Cover: in the theatre: He/she can go on and do either the leading part or several of them, without actually stepping foot on the stage. They can walk after the interval.(home)

Spotlight and Contacts are the actor's and casting director's works of daily reference. Who, why, when and where. From 7 Leicester Place near the Square, London.

PCR is a similar publication to let people know who is about to make what.

EMF: It is a classification of the kinds of home one can put one's mother in when the time comes. She's very happy there and has many friends, I visit her once a week and this book is dedicated to her. She is a wonderful woman, she is 93, should used to be able to add up a column of figures, without ever once making an error and almost instantly. She can't do that now but luckily she can't remember that she ever did. She's fine, thanks for asking.

Philistines: People that seem to deal with sensitive issues very crudely. You might be thinking that I am one of these. (in fact, the Philistines were a very cultured lot... though they never had Strictly Come Dancing!) Everything I say in this book can be interpreted very superficially... that's up to you.. but I want you to know that I really care about the business of acting and the business of TV. (and films and theatre and mothers) It is essential you ignore all the advice in this book... apart from that which is relevant to you.

That's a Wrap!------------ Time to wrap up the circus and put it in a bag and send it off to the post production suite or to the chemist. They might be specific and say 'that's a wrap for Mr Bennett.. thank you very much...' and it is!

The end.